THE VIA DOLOROSA
A FORENSIC AND SPIRITUAL TREATISE ON THE SALVIFIC WORK OF JESUS CHRIST

Michael L. Russo

Copyright © 2013 by Michael L. Russo

THE VIA DOLOROSA
A FORENSIC AND SPIRITUAL TREATISE ON THE
SALVIFIC WORK OF JESUS CHRIST
by Michael L. Russo

Printed in the United States of America

ISBN 9781625097033

All rights reserved solely by the author. The author guarantees all contents are original and do not infringe upon the legal rights of any other person or work. No part of this book may be reproduced in any form without the permission of the author. The views expressed in this book are not necessarily those of the publisher.

Unless otherwise indicated, Bible quotations are taken from The New American Bible. Copyright © 1990 by Oxford University Press.

The designer used the hand print to make the connection that Jesus Christ was on earth for a small amount of time physically. During His time he made an impact that "touched" people's lives spiritually, physically and mentally.

www.xulonpress.com

*For my wife, Nancy, whose love, support,
and encouragement helped me
to achieve goals that I thought were beyond my reach.*

*For my son, Michael, whose gentle
but firm inquiries about my progress
kept my nose to the grindstone
and for his invaluable assistance
as my roving photographer.*

*For my mentor and advisor, Rev. Patrick Cronauer, O.S.B.,
whose enthusiasm, guidance, and attention to detail
challenged me on many levels.*

CONTENTS

TABLE OF ILLUSTRATIONS
ABBREVIATIONS

CHAPTERS

	Introduction	xiii
1	The Via Dolorosa	17
2	Pontius Pilate	27
3	The Antonia Fortress	34
4	Jerusalem and the Via Dolorosa	39
5	The Garden of Gethsemane	45
6	The Stations of the Cross	54
7	The First Station: Jesus Is Condemned to Death	61
8	The Second Station: Jesus Carries His Cross	81
9	The Third Station: Jesus Falls for the First Time	88
10	The Fourth Station: Jesus Meets His Mother	92
11	The Fifth Station: Simon of Cyrene Helps Jesus	96
12	The Sixth Station: Veronica Wipes the Face of Jesus	99
13	The Seventh Station: Jesus Falls for the Second Time	102
14	The Eighth Station: Meets the Women of Jerusalem	105

15	The Ninth Station: Jesus Falls for the Third Time	109
16	The Tenth Station: Jesus Is Stripped of His Garments	114
17	The Eleventh Station: Jesus Is Nailed to the Cross	119
18	The Twelfth Station: Jesus Dies on the Cross	132
19	The Thirteenth Station: Jesus Is Taken Down from the Cross	146
20	The Tomb in a Garden	149
21	The *Aedicule*	158
22	The Tomb of Christ	161
23	The Fourteenth Station: Jesus Is Laid in the Tomb	166
	Conclusion	173
	WORKS CITED	175
	ELECTRONIC WORKS CITED	183

TABLE OF ILLUSTRATIONS

FIGURE

1	Two Street Maps Showing the Path of the Via Dolorosa	24
2	A First-Century CE Limestone Block Identifying Pontius Pilate	31
3	A Replica of the Antonia Fortress	38
4	Three Examples of Akkadian Cuneiform Tablets	40
5	A Map of the Jerusalem Area in the First Century CE	46
6	The Garden of Gethsemane	47
7	The Cave of the Garden of Gethsemane	48

Contents

8	A Map Illustrating the Location of the Omariye College, the Chapel of Condemnation, and the Chapel of Flagellation	65
9	The Chapel of Condemnation and the Altar of the Chapel	66
10	An Illustration of Scourging	70
11	The Ecce Homo Arch and the Stone Pavement	73
12	Crucifixion Evidence	77
13	Ossuary Inscription Identifying Crucifixion Victim	78
14	Illustration of the *Patibulum*, *Crux Commissa*, and *Titulus*	84
15	Examples of First-Century CE Crosses	84
16	Illustrations of Various Methods of Carrying the Cross	86
17	Interior and Exterior Views of the Second Station of the Cross	91
18	The Lintel and Chapel at the Fourth Station of the Cross	94
19	The Location Where It Is Believed Simon of Cyrene Helped Jesus	98
20	The Column Marking Where Veronica Wiped the Face of Jesus	101
21	The Judgment Gate	104
22	The Cardo Maximus	104
23	The Marker Identifying Where Jesus Met the Women of Jerusalem	108
24	The Column Marking the Ninth Station of the Cross and the Ethiopian Monastery	112
25	The Basileus Game Etched into the Lithostrotos Pavement	117
26	Courtyard of the Chapel of the Franks and Stairs to Golgotha	118

27	Artist Renditions of the Crucifixion of Jesus Christ	121
28	An Illustration Showing How Christ's Hands Were Nailed to the Cross Cross	123
29	An Illustration Showing How Christ's Feet Were Nailed to the Cross	128
30	A Painting of the Crucifixion by Peter Paul Rubens	129
31	The Mosaic of Jesus Being Nailed to the Cross	130
32	The Staircase Leading to Calvary and Golgotha Protected from Tourists	142
33	The Chapel of Adam and a View of the Cracked Portion of Golgotha	143
34	The Main Altar over the Crucifixion Site	144
35	A Wide-Angle View of the Altar at the Crucifixion Site	145
36	The Altar of Our Lady of Sorrows	148
37	An Illustration of a Tomb Belonging to a Wealthy Family	150
38	An Illustration of an Arcosolium	151
39	Gordon's Imagined Topography of Jerusalem	152
40	The Garden Tomb	155
41	The Aedicule	160
42	The Rotunda of the *Aedicule* and the Tomb of Christ	164
43	The Chapel of the Angel and Entrance to Christ's Tomb	165
44	The Chapel of the Angel "Stone" and Entrance Sign to Christ's Tomb	171

ABBREVIATIONS

ABD	*The Anchor Bible Dictionary*
BAS	*Biblical Archaeology Society*
BTBA	*Biblica: The Bible Atlas*
EDB	*Eerdmans Dictionary of the Bible*
NAB	*New American Bible*
NJBC	*New Jerome Biblical Commentary*

INTRODUCTION

This project focusing on the Via Dolorosa can be summed up for me in one word, and that word is "transforming." Initially, the project was all about research. I gathered the graphics and the historical information and began to structure my vision for the project. As I moved from research to project structure, I was transformed from research to reflection. As the pieces of the puzzle came together, I found myself reflecting on Jesus, what He did for me, and what He did for all humanity. I discovered that my quest for a deeper understanding of the salvific work of Jesus Christ was opening my mind and my heart to new levels of interest that I, heretofore, had never explored. Again, I was transformed. My reflections changed into meditation as I mentally placed myself on the Via Dolorosa and walked alongside Christ.

I found myself in a mode of reading in which I was not only gathering information but reflecting on how I would have felt if I had been present on the walk to the cross. My mind then moved from the past to the present as I wrestled with a myriad of feelings. Finally, there were times when

The Via Dolorosa

my meditation transformed itself into *Lectio Divina*.[1] I could hear the conversation between Jesus and Pilate, the screams and jeers of the crowd, the quiet sobs of His mother, and the last words that Jesus spoke. I could hear Jesus speaking to me. In short, this project transformed into a learning experience, an emotional experience, and a spiritual experience for me. Hopefully, it will also do the same for those who read it for personal reflection!

In view of the above, I would like to share my goals for our time together on the Via Dolorosa. The historical information that I provide will add greater depth and understanding to the Passion and death of Christ. It will bring the reader to the Via Dolorosa in a manner that creates an atmosphere of actually walking to Calvary with Jesus. It is my hope that, in understanding the events surrounding the crucifixion of Christ, the examples and explanations that I provide will expose the reader to some elements of Christ's Passion and death that he or she has never experienced before. By so doing, I hope to provide a tool for drawing oneself closer to God.

The entire account of the Passion is set in five different locations. It begins in the Garden of Gethsemane on the Mount of Olives, and continues in the palace of the

---

[1] According to Michael Casey, *Lectio Divina* is more than the pious perusal of "spiritual books." *Lectio Divina* is a technique of prayer and a guide to living. It is a means of descending to the level of the heart and of finding God. Michael Casey, *Sacred Reading: The Art of Lectio Divina* (Liguori, MO: Liguori Publications, 1996), vi. Thelma Hall refers to *Lectio* as a "holistic way of prayer which disposes, opens and 'in-forms' us for the gift of contemplation God wants to give, by leading us to a meeting place with Him in our deepest center, His life-giving dwelling place. It begins this movement by introducing us to the power of the word of God in Scripture to speak to the most intimate depths of our hearts, to gift and challenge and change us, and to promote genuine spiritual growth and maturity." Thelma Hall, R.C., *Too Deep for Words: Rediscovering Lectio Divina* (Mahwah, NJ: Paulist Press, 1988), 7.

Introduction

retired high priest Annas where the scribes and the elders were gathered. Scripture tells us that the chief priests and the entire Sanhedrin were trying to obtain false testimony against Jesus so that they could put Him to death (Matt. 26:57, 59; Mark 14:53–55; Luke 22:54; John 18:12). When Jesus was finally declared guilty of blasphemy, He was held overnight in prison so that the chief priests and elders could take counsel about their decision.

The decision was ratified by the morning, and the event moved to Pilate's palace. Because it was not lawful for the Jews to put any man to death, they put the trial into Pilate's hands (John 18:31). Pilate struggled with making a decision, but in the end, he gave in and condemned Jesus to death, just as the Jews had demanded. Jesus was then taken from the Praetorium to Golgotha where the execution sentence was carried out. The Passion and death of Jesus concludes in a garden where the burial takes place. This suffices to show that the account is built according to concentric structure. The story within a story surrounds and draws attention to a central theme: the kingship of Christ. The theological importance of the Roman trial cannot be ignored, for it is during the trial before Pilate that the theme of Christ's kingship is developed (Matt. 27:11; Mark 15:2). This scene is situated in the center of the story.

A careful examination of the two garden scenes shows that they do not really belong to the story of the Passion. They respectively provide bookends for the Passion as an introduction and an epilogue. The events of the Passion itself take place in the three inner scenes they enclose: the interrogation before Annas, the Roman trial, and Golgotha.[2] The Passion of Christ will be studied in both a theological and

---

[2] Ignace De La Potterie, SJ, *The Hour of Jesus: The Passion and the Resurrection of Jesus According to John* (Staten Island, NY: Alba House, 1997), 24.

a technical presentation. Pierre Barbet suggests that prior to his book *A Doctor at Calvary*, which was published in 1953, theologians and exegetes had difficulty describing the sufferings of Christ because they scarcely understood them. He claims that proof of this can be found in many of the traditional sermons that were shared with the faithful prior to his book. Barbet tells a story about his friend, Dr. Pasteau, the president of the Société de Saint-Luc of Catholic Doctors in France. Dr. Pasteau was visiting the Vatican with several high dignitaries of the church. Referencing Barbet's research, he explained how much we now know about the death of Jesus and His terrible sufferings. Pasteau discussed how Jesus suffered from cramps in all His muscles and died from asphyxia. Cardinal Pacelli (who became Pope Pius XII) and the others went pale with grief and compassion. The cardinal replied, "We did not know; nobody ever told us that."[3]

---

[3] Pierre Barbet, MD, *A Doctor at Calvary* (Fort Collins, CO: Roman Catholic Books, 1953), 7–8.

CHAPTER 1

THE VIA DOLOROSA

Son though He was, He learned obedience through what He suffered; and when He was made perfect, He became the source of eternal salvation for all who obey Him. (Heb. 5:8–9)[4]

The Via Dolorosa at [sic] Jerusalem (though it was not called that name before the sixteenth century) was reverently marked out from the earliest times and has been the goal of pious pilgrims ever since the days of Constantine. Tradition asserts that the Blessed Virgin used to visit the scenes of Christ's Passion daily and St. Jerome speaks of the crowds of pilgrims from all countries which used to visit the holy places in his day.[5]

There is no evidence that any specific forms of special devotion took place at each of the stations at such an

---

[4] Unless otherwise indicated, all translations are taken from *The Catholic Study Bible: The New American Bible* (New York: Oxford University Press), 1990.

[5] George C. Alston, "Way of the Cross, Stations of the Cross," in *The Catholic Encyclopedia*, vol. 15 (New York: Robert Appleton Company, 1912). http://newadvent.org/ cathen/5569a.htm.

early date. However, before Constantine's time, Christian pilgrims did visit the Holy Land to pay their respects to the birthplace of their religion. There were a limited number of sites at that time because many were buried under the ruins left by the destruction of Jerusalem in 70 CE or lay "under the structures raised by Hadrian when he built a Palestinian [sic] centre, 'Aelia Capitolina' upon the remains of the old city of Jerusalem."[6]

Hadrian's desire to build a pagan city on the site of Jewish Jerusalem may have been one of the reasons that sparked the revolt in 131–132 CE. He set a temple to Jupiter on the site of the Lord's temple. The Jews were outraged, and their revolt quickly gained support. The Romans quickly put down the revolt, and to put a definitive end to Jewish hopes of restoration, the Romans built the new city of Aelia Capitolina on the site of Jewish Jerusalem. Aelius was Hadrian's family name. Capitolina was the most sacred shrine in the Roman Empire. It was a temple in Rome dedicated to the gods of the Mons Capitolium.[7]

The earliest recorded Christian traveler to the Holy Land was Melito of Sardis (190 CE), a pilgrim whose interests in the Holy Land were twofold, namely, historical inquiry and preaching. Because the Gnostics denied both the physical humanity of Christ and the unity of the Old and New Testament dispensations, it was important for Melito to accurately establish the books of the Old Testament and to identify the locations of the scriptural references of the Lord's incarnate life.[8] Alexander and Firmilian, both bishops of Cappodocian

---

[6] Lionel Casson, *Travel in the Ancient World* (Baltimore, MD: Johns Hopkins University Press, 1994), 304.

[7] Robert T. Wilken, *The Land Called Holy* (New Haven, CT: Yale University Press, 1992), 42–43.

[8] Duncan Macpherson, *Pilgrim Preacher: Palestine, Pilgrimage, and Preacher* (Trowbridge, England: Cromwell Press, 2004), 17.

towns, and Origen also made visits to the Holy Land.[9] Alexander journeyed to the Holy Land in 212 CE to pray and to investigate the holy places.[10] There is a manuscript written by St. Sylvia of Aquitaine in 380 CE (*Peregrinatio ad loca sancta*) that describes the minute details of every religious devotion in the Holy Land, yet fails to mention any devotion to the Stations of the Cross.[11] Various articles identify St. Sylvia with Egeria, a famous Christian pilgrim to the Holy Land between 381 CE and 384 CE.[12] None of the early pilgrims make any reference to the Stations of the Cross or to any specific devotions associated with them. The earliest use of the word "Stations" occurs in the narrative of an English pilgrim, William Wey, who visited the Holy Land in 1458 and again in 1462. He described the manner in which the "Stations of the Cross" were followed at that time. He observed that the general practice was to begin at Mount Calvary and proceed backward to Pilate's house. The more "reasonable way" of traveling the route to Calvary was adopted only in the early part of the sixteenth century. It was determined that the route should begin at Pilate's house and end at Mount Calvary.[13]

---

[9] Casson, *Travel in the Ancient World*, 304.

[10] Rev. William Edward Scudamore, MA, "Holy Places," in *A Dictionary of Christian Antiquities*, vol.1 (Hartford, England: J.B. Burr Publishing Co., 1880), 774.

[11] Alston, "Way of the Cross."

[12] Egeria describes her pilgrimage and the liturgy she found in Jerusalem. She wrote to her "Sisters." It is not clear whether her sisters were Christian acquaintances and friends or members of a religious community. It is believed that she came from Spain as did St. Sylvia of Aquitaine. John Wilkinson, *Egeria's Travels* (Oxford: Oxbow Books, 1999), 1.

[13] During the fifteenth and sixteenth centuries several reproductions of holy places were set up in different parts of Europe. In these early examples, an attempt was made to reproduce the most hallowed spots on the Via Dolorosa. Alston, "Way of the Cross."

Pilgrimages greatly developed throughout the Byzantine period (324–640 CE). The building of shrines was extensive and many were erected over the supposed holy sites. It is a tremendous challenge for biblical scholars to identify the sacred places mentioned in the Bible. Although there are some areas that are easy to identify such as Jerusalem, Damascus, and Rome, other cities and sites must rely on specialists in historical geography and archaeology for identification. This is a painstaking process and involves careful study of Biblical references. Even the most skeptical scholars agree that the Bible is very accurate about geography. Ancient itineraries and location descriptions are carefully studied to get a rough idea of an exact location.

> The study of history is not merely the study of a series of facts. It is an attempt to understand the past in all its complexity and variation through the written documents of past people. Archaeology is also the study of the past, but through the material culture of ancient peoples.
>
> The Bible is a detailed account of the people and places of the time. Its readers were familiar with the geography, cultural practices, and history referred to, but modern readers lack this familiarity.[14]

Scholars assume that the most ancient areas are buried beneath the sites in Jerusalem. Archaeological excavations have uncovered intricate water systems dating back to the period of the Divided Monarchy. Archaeologist Kathleen Kenyon uncovered what may be the fortification walls of Jerusalem from the time of the United Monarchy.[15] The

---

[14] Barry J. Beitzel, chief consultant and others, "Geography and History of the Bible Lands," in *Biblica: The Bible Atlas* (Hauppauge, NY: Barron's Educational Series, 2007), 31.

[15] Ibid., 62.

search for sites mentioned in the Gospels has been an ongoing project for centuries. For example, before 130 CE, Justin Martyr was told of the cave in Bethlehem where Jesus was born.[16]

The beginning of scientific archaeological research can be credited to Edward Robinson in the early nineteenth century. Because of his knowledge of biblical history and biblical Hebrew, he was uniquely qualified to study the ancient sites. By 1838 he and Eli Smith identified more than one hundred major sites mentioned in the Bible. This was partly because Smith was fluent in Arabic, and many of the villages retained traces of their ancient names. Although Robinson pioneered the discipline of historical geography, archaeology was his weakest tool, and his lack of archaeological experience left him unsophisticated in the field of archaeological exploration. It appears that Robinson did not even understand the nature of a tell and failed to recognize important sites.[17] Digging archaeologically demands that careful attention be paid to the multiple layers that exist at a certain site. New cities and civilizations were once built upon earlier ones, and excavation is a long and tedious process of exposing each layer. The technical term for this is the *strati-*

---

[16] M. C. Tenney and J. I. Packer, *Illustrated Manners and Customs of the Bible* (Nashville, TN: Thomas Nelson Publishers, 1980), 105.

[17] Thomas E. Levy, "Archaeology and the Bible," in *Eerdmans Dictionary of the Bible*, ed. David Noel Freedman (Grand Rapids, MI: William B. Eerdmans Publishing Company, 2000), 90. A tell (also tel) is a settlement in the form of a mound. It is often found in an otherwise level countryside. Related words are *tepe*, *huyuk*, and *khirbet*. Tells are the result of a specific type of architecture known as mud brick. Mudbrick architecture is fairly durable when it is properly maintained. However, it must be torn down and rebuilt often. A tell is formed when this happens, and when abandoned structures disintegrate, new ones are constructed directly on top of their remains. Each successive building phase is on a raised surface. The result is the formation of a mound, or a tell. Katherine A. Mackay, "Tell (also Tel)," *EDB*, 1279.

graph approach.[18] There are different ways that archaeologists and historians discuss sites in the Holy Land. Sites are considered to be traditional sites because there are no hard records such as maps and documents that clearly identify the exact location. Archaeologists have discovered that an octagonal church would have been built on the location of a traditional site to mark the holy site. This is valuable information for determining the authenticity of a particular site or location. There are different levels of certitude for identifying the various sites recognized by the pilgrims. Pilgrims may have erected shrines because they recognized a specific location as being sacred. Other sites are identified as authentic because an ancient structure such as a church was discovered on the site.

"Pilgrims participated in liturgical celebrations at the shrines, often joining the indigenous faithful who identified and developed most of the pilgrimage sites. Participating in Holy Week and Easter celebrations, as well as the Christmas feast at Bethlehem, was extremely popular. These celebrations provided ample opportunity for highly-charged liturgical preaching as is evident in the sermons of Cyril of Jerusalem, the first Bishop of Jerusalem to preside at the Liturgy in the Church of the Holy Sepulchre."[19]

Today, the Via Dolorosa, also called the "Way of Sorrows," leads from the site of the Praetorium to the Church of the Holy Sepulchre. There is, however, considerable debate as to the actual location of the Via Dolorosa. Hershel Shanks, editor of the *Biblical Archeology Review*, states that none of the various locations argued to be the beginning of the

---

[18] John Dominic Crossan, Jonathan L. Reed. *Excavating Jesus: Beneath the Stones, Behind the Texts* (New York: Harper Collins Publishers, 2001), xvii.

[19] Macpherson, *Pilgrim Preacher: Palestine, Pilgrimage, and Preacher*, 20.

Via Dolorosa hold up under careful scrutiny.[20] The Sisters of Zion initially identified the place where Pilate judged Jesus, and this was confirmed by Father Louis Hugues Vincent, a French authority on Jerusalem. Father Pierre Benoit, another well-known French scholar from the École Biblique, challenged the findings.[21] The Benedictine monk, Father Bargil Pixner, confirmed that there are difficult problems identifying the location where Jesus stood before Pilate.[22] Father Jerome Murphy-O'Connor, also of the École Biblique, wrote: "The Via Dolorosa is defined by faith, not by history."[23] Sister Brigitte Martin-Chave of the Sisters of Zion Convent adds, "Through pilgrimage, the convent acquired a sanctity that

---

[20] Hershel Shanks claims that "the Via Dolorosa, 'the Way of Tears,' was the route Jesus followed from imprisonment to Calvary, where He was crucified. The Ecce Homo Arch crosses the Via Dolorosa at the Second Station, in front of the Sisters of Zion Convent in the Old City. In the basement of the convent is a polished stone pavement, which was long thought to be the *Lithostrotos*, the stone pavement where Jesus is said to have been judged by Pontius Pilate. The Ecce Homo Arch is the place on the route where Pilate proclaimed, 'Behold the Man' (John 19:5). Alas, none of these identifications holds up under careful scrutiny." Hershel Shanks, *Jerusalem: An Archaeological Biography* (New York, NY: Random House, 1995), 189.

[21] Ibid., 193.

[22] Bargil Pixner, OSB, was responsible for introducing the Dormition Abbey's theology students to archeology and biblical topography. As an archeologist, Father Pixner is well versed in the knowledge of the Holy Land and its history. While he agrees that there is difficulty locating where Jesus began His walk to Calvary, he clearly states, "The point of departure was the Lithostrotos with the colored pavement in front of the Hasmonean Palace. In my opinion, this was located where the German Knights later built their St. Mary's Church, the ruins of which can be seen today inside the archaeological garden facing the Temple area in the Jewish Quarter. Here the original Via Dolorosa began." Bargil Pixner, OSB, *With Jesus in Jerusalem, His First and Last Days in Judea* (Israel: Corazin Publishing, 1996) 122, 137.

[23] Shanks, *Jerusalem: An Archaeological Biography*, 189.

The Via Dolorosa

history may not have bestowed upon it. This site has been made holy by the prayers that have been offered over the years."[24]

"The Via Dolorosa is a diagonal path which runs across the city from the Gate of St. Stephen to the Holy Sepulchre."[25] There are fourteen Stations of the Cross along the Via Dolorosa; nine are located along the route itself. Of these nine, only eight are today indicated by various churches and shrines. Five Stations of the Cross are located inside the Church of the Holy Sepulchre.[26]

Figure 1. Two views of the Via Dolorosa. **Left:** This illustration identifies the number and approximate location of each Station of the Cross along the route. **Right:** This illustration reveals only the path from the Gate of St. Stephen to the Church of the Holy Sepulchre and does not identify any Stations of the Cross.[27]

A chapel was erected in the southern part of the courtyard of the first Station during the Crusader period, but it

---

[24] Ibid., 195–196. This discussion will continue when addressing the Antonia Fortress.

[25] Edward Wilson, *In Scripture Lands: New Views of Sacred Places* (London: The Religious Tract Society, 1891), 203.

[26] Y. Salomon and M. Milner, *Jesus 2000* (Israel: Alpha Communication Ltd., 1998) 193.

[27] Left photo: Public Domain, http://commons.wikimedia.org/wiki/File:Plan_via_crucis_Jerusalem.JPG. Right photo: Todd Bolden/BblePlaces.com, Byzantine Jerusalem model, Temple Mount, tb082305546.

The Via Dolorosa

was destroyed in an earthquake in 1927.[28] Although the debate continues concerning the exact beginning of the Via Dolorosa, Father Pixner suggested that "We should nevertheless, for our devotions, remain loyal to the old venerable Way of the Cross, already a custom for more than five centuries. Its last station (Golgotha) has been scientifically established, though its beginning has not."[29] Golgotha was first mentioned as being the site of Jesus's crucifixion by 135 CE and was officially recognized as such by the Emperor Constantine after 325 CE.[30]

The Holy Land attracts Christians from all over the world, and one could view its religious significance as a catalyst for unity. However, this has not been the case when it comes to ownership.

> The Greek Orthodox, Roman Catholic, and Armenian Orthodox churches are known as *major* communities, with rights of possession and usage at the holy places. The Coptic, Ethiopian, and Syrian Orthodox churches are deemed *minor* communities with rights of usage but not rights of possession at the holy places. Since the Crusades, Greeks and Latins (as Greek Orthodox and Roman Catholics are known in Jerusalem) have been locked in a fierce struggle over their family home—the Church of the Holy Sepulchre.[31]

---

[28] The courtyard refers to the Omariye College, which was built in the Mameluke period (1250 CE –1517 CE) over the foundations of the Antonia Fortress. See Salomon and Milner, *Jesus 2000*, 193.

[29] Pixner, *With Jesus in Jerusalem*, 125.

[30] Tenney and Packer, *Illustrated Manners and Customs*, 105.

[31] Raymond Cohen. *Saving the Holy Sepulchre: How Rival Christians Came to Rescue Their Holiest Shrine* (New York, NY: Oxford University Press, 2008), 5–6.

Another reality of the Holy Land is that it is holy to the three Abrahamic and Semitic faiths—Christianity, Islam, and Judaism.[32]

---

[32] Macpherson, *Pilgrim Preacher*, 55–56. On page 57 of the same work, Macpherson adds the following footnote: "The Greek Orthodox Patriarch of Jerusalem has precedence over other Church leaders. The Greek Orthodox community is the largest Christian denomination in the Holy Land, numbering 27,000 in Jerusalem and the Occupied Territories and approximately 29,000 in Israel proper. If we exclude Egypt with more than ten percent of its population adhering to the Coptic Orthodox Church, it is the most numerous of Christian denominations in the Arab world." The footnote is credited to H. Norman, *A Guide to the Christian Churches in the Middle East* (Elkhart, IN: Mission Focus, 1989), 96–117.

CHAPTER 2

PONTIUS PILATE

Then they brought Jesus from Caiaphas to the Praetorium. It was morning. And they themselves did not enter the Praetorium, in order not to be defiled so that they could eat the Passover. So Pilate came out to them and said, "What charge do you bring against this man?"
(John 19:28–29)

Pilate was appointed to office in the twelfth year of Tiberius's reign by Sejanus, Tiberius's anti-Jewish advisor.[33] He arrived as governor of Judea in 26 CE and reigned as such until 36 CE.[34] "The *praefecti* or *procuratores* were financial and military administrators who ruled the imperial province, dwelt in Herod's palace at Caesarea or Jerusalem, and could call on the legate of Syria for help

---

[33] *Eusebius, The Ecclesiastical History*, vol. 1, Kirsopp Lake translation (London England: Harvard University Press, 1998), 75; Roland E. Murphy, O.Carm, "A History of Israel," #75, §168E, in *The New Jerome Biblical Commentary*, (Upper Saddle River, NJ: Prentice Hall, 1990), 1249.

[34] Walker, *In the Steps of Jesus*, 11. Daniel R. Schwartz, "Pontius Pilate," *ABD*, vol. 5, 396.

if necessary."³⁵ The procurators were of the equestrian order, and as such governors were entrusted with full authority by the emperor, even with the power of capital punishment. The appointment of men to a military prefecture demonstrates the determination of the emperor to bring native inhabitants of a newly subjugated territory under Roman control. The title of prefect that was used under Tiberius was changed under Claudius's rule. Claudius preferred the civilian title "procurator," which elevated the position from a simple fiscal agent to a public official taking on the governmental duties of the former prefect. Egypt was the only place to retain the title of prefect, possibly to indicate the continued military character of the governor.³⁶ The responsibilities of the governor of Judea were primarily military. Before the reign of Agrippa (41–44 CE), the title "prefect" was used (*praefectus*/ἔπαρχος).³⁷

> In New Testament times "governor" (Gk. *hēgemṓn*) usually referred to the ruler of a Roman province (Mark 13:9; 1 Pet. 2:14). Matthew notes that Christians could be hauled into court "before governors and kings" for Christ's sake (Matt. 10:18; cf. Mark 13:9; Luke 21:12). In His trial Jesus was brought before Pilate, the Roman governor of Judea (Matt. 27:2, 11–26).
>
> Three kinds of Roman officials are described as "governors" in Luke: the legate, a military ruler governing an imperial province (Quirinius of Syria, Luke 2:2); the proconsul, governing a senatorial province (Sergius Paulus

---

³⁵ Murphy, "A History of Israel," #75, §167D, in the *NJBC*, 1248; Schwartz, "Pontius Pilate," *ABD*, 397.

³⁶ Helen K. Bond, *Pontius Pilate in History and Interpretation* (New York, NY: Cambridge University Press, 1998), 12.

³⁷ Ibid., 11. Additional information concerning titles and responsibilities can be found in Schwartz, "Pontius Pilate," *ABD*, 397–398.

of Cyprus, Acts 13:7; Gallio of Achaia, 18:12); and the prefect or procurator, governing a subdivision of a province with a settled army (Pontius Pilate, Luke 3:1; Felix, Acts 23:24, Festus, 24:27).[38]

Our chief source of information on Pontius Pilate is Flavius Josephus. The writings of Philo provide additional insight. Josephus indicates that there were several episodes when Pilate showed his antagonistic stance toward Jewish sensitivities. There is a theory that Pilate was inspired by Sejanus, an enormously powerful Praetorian prefect who commanded the troops in Rome that protected the emperor and his family and also maintained strict order. Sejanus is said to have been extremely anti-Semitic and sent Pontius Pilate to Judea as governor in 26 CE to provoke conflict by ignoring Jewish sensitivities.[39] Pontius Pilate had replaced Valerius Gratus as governor and immediately antagonized the Jews when he brought the army from Caesarea to Jerusalem to abolish Jewish laws. He ordered the army to bring Caesar's ensigns into the city at nighttime. The Jews considered the emblem to be an idol, and they rebelled when the soldiers paraded the ensigns through the streets. Although Pilate was prepared to take immediate action, he was impressed with the firm resolution of the people and commanded the images

---

[38] Allison A. Trites, "Governor," *EDB*, 524.

[39] Warren Carter, *Pontius Pilate: Portraits of a Roman Governor* (Collegeville, MN: Liturgical Press, 2003), 3. Carter references others that agree with this view such as Ethelbert Stauffer, *Christ and the Caesars: Historical Sketches*. Translated by K. and R. Gregor Smith (London: S.C.M., 1955); Ernest Bammel, "Syrian Coinage and Pilate," *Journal of Jewish Studies*, vol. 2 (1950–1951) 108–10; Paul Winter, *On the Trial of Jesus* (Berlin: Walter de Gruyter, 1961); Haim Cohn, *The Trial and Death of Jesus* (London: Weidenfeld & Nicholson, 1972); Harold W. Hoehner, "Pilate," *Dictionary of Jesus and the Gospels* (Downers Grove: Intervarsity Press, 1992), 615–16.

to be carried back to Caesarea. On another occasion, Pilate funded the building of an aqueduct with money that was to be used for the Temple. In the ensuing riot, he sent his soldiers into the crowd with hidden daggers, which they used when he gave the signal.[40]

According to W. Carter, Philo used Pilate as an example of how not to rule over the Jews. Philo is very careful to demonstrate that the Jewish opposition was not to the emperor or to Roman rule in general. Philo presents the Emperor Tiberius as one who honors and protects Jewish traditions. He presents Pilate in a completely opposite and negative view.[41] In 36 CE, Pilate put down a Samaritan revolt in such a barbaric fashion that the Samaritans complained to the legate of Syria, Vitellius, who demanded that Pilate travel to Rome to respond to the charges made by the Jews. Upon hearing the reports, the Emperor Tiberius was appalled and recalled Pilate to Rome.[42]

Ironically, until June 1961, there was no archaeological evidence for Pontius Pilate's existence. Then, an inscription was discovered in the first-century CE theater at Caesarea Maritima with a clear reference in Latin to Pontius Pilate. The inscription block had been reused as a step in the theater during repairs made in the late Roman period. It had originally been part of a dedicatory plaque for a Tiberium,

---

[40] Josephus provides information about Pontius Pilate to support the statements that Pilate was a ruthless leader who had little regard and less patience for the Jews. William Whiston, *The New Complete Works of Josephus* (Grand Rapids MI: Kregel Publications, 1999), *Jewish Antiquities* 3.1. 2 and *Jewish Antiquities* 2.9.4. Additional information can also be found in *NJBC*, Murphy, "A History of Israel," #75, §167–168, 1248–9.

[41] Carter, *Pontius Pilate*, 16.

[42] Whiston, *New Complete Works of Josephus*, 592. Reference of Pilate's recall to Rome is also found in Walker, *In the Steps of Jesus*, 87 and Schwartz, "Pontius Pilate," 395–401.

that is, a structure erected in honor of the Emperor Tiberius. In this instance, the structure was believed to be a temple. The inscription read, "Pontius Pilate, the Prefect of Judea, has dedicated to the people of Caesarea a temple in honor of Tiberius."[43]

Figure 2. **Left:** The actual limestone block that was discovered in a first-century theater. **Right:** The example of the inscription with the missing letters filled in.[44]

Several scholars have assumed that the Tiberium was a temple dedicated to Tiberius. However, because the inscription is in such poor condition, it is impossible to verify the type of building. Because of the small size of the block, some scholars believe that its purpose was for recording the name of a secular building.[45]

---

[43] BAS, *Biblical World in Pictures* (Washington DC: Biblical Archaeological Review, 2006 CD), photo SNT52.

[44] Michael L. Russo. Photographed by Michael James Russo, April 20, 2012.

[45] Bond, *Pontius Pilate in History*, 12.

The type of building is not important for this work. The important issue concerning the discovery of the block is that it confirms that Pilate was in Palestine at the time of Christ's Passion and death. The first line of the block links Pilate to Tiberius, the emperor from 14–37 CE. This first line suggests that the inscription marks an attempt to honor Tiberius (and possibly Pilate) in some way. The second line names Pontius Pilate, and the third line identifies him as prefect or governor of Judea.[46] There are many references to Pontius Pilate in the Gospels and in Philo, Flavius Josephus, and Eusebius.[47] These provide us with a glimpse of Pilate's personality but do not provide enough background information to develop a composite of his personality. The references in Josephus and Philo help to expand our knowledge of the man, but information about Pilate is not extensive.[48]

Pilate probably spent most of his time in Caesarea, the administrative capital of the provinces, only coming to Jerusalem on business and at critical times such as Passover. The discovery of the inscription caused quite a debate because it identifies Pilate as Praefectus and not Procurator. "Prefect" was the governor's title until the time of Claudius (41–54 CE), who changed it to "Procurator."[49] The term *Praefectus*, and its Greek equivalent ($\dot{\varepsilon}\pi\alpha\rho\chi o\varsigma$) are often used

---

[46] Carter, *Pontius Pilate*, 13.

[47] See Matt. 27:1–2, 11–26; Mark 15:1–15; Luke 23:25; John 18:28–40, 19:1–22; Philo, "Embassy to Gaius" in *Philo*. 10 vols. Vol 9. Translated by F.H. Colson Loeb Classical Library (Cambridge, MA: Harvard University Press, 1941); Flavius Josephus, "The Life Against Apion," "The Jewish War," and "Jewish Antiquities." *Josephus*. 9 vols. Translated by H. St. J. Thackeray, MA, Ralph Marcus, and Louis H. Feldman. Loeb Classical Library (Cambridge, MA: Harvard University Press, 1926-1963).

[48] Carter, *Pontius Pilate*, 12.

[49] Claudius demonstrated excellent management. Among his accomplishments during his reign, he established a government bureau-

interchangeably with procurator and its Greek equivalent (έπροπος) to denote governors. The term *prefect* has a military origin. The term *procurator* is a civilian term. The terms *governor*, *prefect*, and *procurator* attest to Pilate's role as the representative of Rome's ruling elite.[50] It is impossible to say what really happened to Pontius Pilate after he was recalled by Tiberius. Legend has it that he committed suicide because he fell into disfavor. Eusebius writes that Pilate committed suicide because he fell from grace under Caligula.[51] Other legends indicate that Pilate may have come from Germany. The Abyssinian Church in Ethiopia, claiming that he converted to Christianity, named him a saint and June 25 as his feast day.[52] The Coptics ranked Pilate as a martyr. Claudia Procula, Pilate's wife, was thought to have converted to Christianity, as mentioned by Origen. The Greek Church has given Claudia Procula October 27 as a feast day.[53] None of these legends can be validated. However, both the Ethiopic and Coptic churches count Pontius Pilate among their saints.[54]

---

cracy to further facilitate efficient and fair administration of the provinces. John F. Hall, Scott Nash. "Claudius" *EDB*, 262.

[50] Carter, *Pontius Pilate*, 44. Schwartz, "Pontius Pilate," *ABD*, 397.

[51] *Eusebius: The Ecclesiastical History*, vol. 1, Kirsopp Lake translation, 125.

[52] A. Barnes, "Pontius Pilate," in *The Catholic Encyclopedia*. www.newadvent.org/cathen/12083c.htm.

[53] Matthew Bunson, "Pontius Pilate (d. after 37)," in *Our Sunday Visitor's Encyclopedia of Catholic History* (Huntington, IN: Our Sunday Visitor Publishing Division, 1995), 663.

[54] Schwartz, "Pontius Pilate," 400.

CHAPTER 3

THE ANTONIA FORTRESS

> *Then the soldiers of the governor took Jesus inside the Praetorium and gathered the whole cohort around him. And kneeling before him, they mocked him, saying, "Hail, King of the Jews!" They spat upon Him and kept striking Him on the head. (Matt. 27:27–30)*

The Antonia Fortress was built by Herod in 10 BCE in honor of Mark Antony who had crowned Herod King of Judea. The Antonia served as a base for the Roman garrison in Jerusalem, the seat of the Roman governor, and as the courthouse—known as the Praetorium.[55] The structure is called the "castle" in Acts 31:34.[56] The Antonia Fortress also served as a palace, and many scholars believe it was the place where Jesus's trial before Pilot took place. Others

---

[55] Salomon and Milner, *Jesus 2000*, 192.

[56] Various Bible translations refer to the "castle," the "compound," or other titles in Acts 21:34. The *NAB* uses the word "compound." For the "castle" reference see Tenney and Packer, *Illustrated Manners*, 633. The King James Version uses the term "castle;" both the New Catholic Version and the New International Version use the term "barracks," while the Catholic Living Bible refers to the area as the "armory."

The Antonia Fortress

believe that Pontius Pilate would have been staying in the Roman garrison that overlooked the Temple from the north. Roman troops were increased in Jerusalem during the feasts and were stationed at the Antonia Fortress, which guarded Herod's temple. In addition, they were stationed in Herod's palace to keep order among the Jewish sects and the pilgrims.[57] This concern would explain the presence of Pontius Pilate in Jerusalem at that time. His usual residence was in Caesarea Maritima.[58]

Because visits to Jerusalem were usually scheduled so that the Jews could be monitored and kept from creating an uprising during feast days, Pilate did not look forward to his visits to Jerusalem, and it is unlikely that he would have inconvenienced himself by staying in army barracks. As long as his protection was assured, he most likely used the spacious accommodations in the palace. A sufficient number of the Sanhedrin council members would have easily fit into the spacious courtyards found in the wealthy houses of the Upper City.[59] Bargil Pixner states that Pilate, his wife, his entourage of servants, and his bodyguards used to reside in Herod's Upper Palace when visiting Jerusalem.[60]

Flavius Josephus provides a detailed description of the Antonia Fortress. He describes the walls as being smooth so that no one could climb them. In addition, he states that the inside of the fortress was the size and shape of a palace and was divided into many rooms. Courts and places for bathing as well as large spaces for camps were part of the interior of the fortress. The Antonia Fortress had all the conveniences of several cities, even though it appeared to be a palace. This leads one to believe that once inside the Antonia, there was

---

[57] Walker, *In the Steps of Jesus*, 136.
[58] Salomon and Milner, *Jesus 2000*, 192–193.
[59] Walker, *In the Steps of Jesus*, 162.
[60] Pixner, *With Jesus in Jerusalem*, 122.

no need to visit shops and services in the city because there were sufficient businesses and personal services within the compound to meet every need. Although the Antonia had all the amenities needed for a royal compound, it was still a fortress, and a Roman legion was always on guard to watch over the Temple and the people so that uprisings could be suppressed.[61] A legion is described as having 4,800 men, which consisted of 10 cohorts of 480 men.[62]

The exact location of the Praetorium has been debated for centuries. In the opinion of respected archaeologist Bargil Pixner, "One of the most difficult topographical problems of Jerusalem is to identify the location of the Praetorium, where Jesus stood before the procurator and set out carrying the cross to Golgotha."[63] Actually, the exact location of the Praetorium could have been in one of three palaces used by Herod the Great: the Antonia Fortress, the royal palace of the Hasmoneans, or the new Upper City palace of Herod. Since Crusader times, the Antonia Fortress was identified as the Praetorium.

However, recent archaeological discoveries reveal that the fourteen Stations of the Cross and the beginning of the

---

[61] In book five of the *Jewish Wars*, Josephus provides an elaborate description of the Antonia Fortress by identifying the many towers and the actual sizes of each. His description includes the protective elements of the fortress as well as the elaborate living space. Whiston, *The New Complete Works of Josephus*, *The Jewish War*, 5.5.8.

[62] There are various articles concerning the size of the Roman army. Suffice it to say that the size of a legion ranged from 4,800 men to 6,000 men. A cohort ranged from 480 men to 600 men. A Roman legion was comprised of 10 cohorts. See G. J. Goldberg, "The Roman Army: Key Concepts," (London: Greenhill Books, 1998). http://www.members.aol.com/FlJosephus2/romanArmy.htm. See also "The Roman Army." http://library.thinkquest.org22866/English/Leger.html.

[63] Pixner, *With Jesus in Jerusalem*, 122.

The Antonia Fortress

Via Dolorosa could not have been at the Crusader location.[64] According to Pixner, although Jesus's path probably did not pass along the Via Dolorosa as it is identified today, "We should nevertheless, for our devotions, remain loyal to the old venerable Way of the Cross, already in custom for more than five centuries."[65] Today, the Muslim Omariye College,[66] built during the Mameluke Period (1250–1517 CE) is located in the Antonia compound. The Mamluks erected religious colleges and pilgrim hospices over the huge substructures such as the Antonia Fortress. The word "Mamluk" in Arabic means "owned." This term was applied to boys who were purchased in slave markets and trained to be professional soldiers (specifically, mounted archers). The Mamluks were all forced converts to Islam. Those who emerged from the regiments to leadership roles purchased slaves for themselves who would have no relationship to any other family or political faction. This guaranteed that there would be no conflict of loyalties. The Mamluks were defeated by the Ottoman Turks near Aleppo and Cairo in 1517.[67] The current Omariye College building was constructed on the foundations of the Antonia Fortress built in the Herodian period.[68]

---

[64] Pixner, *With Jesus in Jerusalem*, 122.

[65] Ibid., 125.

[66] Also spelled "Umariyya." Jerome Murphy-O'Connor, OP, *The Holy Land: An Oxford Archaeological Guide from Earliest Times to 1700* (New York: Oxford University Press, 1998), 83.

[67] Murphy-O'Connor, *The Holy Land*, 36. Murphy-O'Connor refers to Mamluks [sic], and Salomon and Milner refer to this period the Mameluke [sic] period.

[68] Salomon and Milner, *Jesus 2000*, 193.

Figure 3. The Antonia Fortress. This portion of the Holy Land Hotel model of Jerusalem shows the square four-towered Antonia Fortress next to the Temple precinct, as described by Josephus (*Jewish War* V, 5).[69]

---

[69] Michael L. Russo. Photographed by Michael James Russo, April 25, 2012.

CHAPTER 4

JERUSALEM AND THE VIA DOLOROSA

> *Behold, we are going to Jerusalem, and the Son of Man will be handed over to the chief priests and the scribes, and they will condemn Him to death, and hand Him over to the Gentiles to be mocked and scourged and crucified.* (Matt. 20:17–19)

*I*n Scripture, Jerusalem is identified by three names, *Jebus* (cf. 1 Chron. 11:4; Judg. 19:10), *Salem* (cf. Ps. 76:2; Gen. 14:18), and *Jerusalem*. In the days of Hadrian, Jerusalem was called Aelia.[70] Historical and archaeological information about the city of Jerusalem is readily available. It is easy to identify the city as the City of David because Scripture is rich with references and images. The New Testament elevates the importance of the city because it was the place where Christ suffered, died, was buried, and rose to life on the third day. "Jerusalem had a long history well

---

[70] John Wilkinson, *Jerusalem Pilgrims before the Crusades* (Warminster, England: Aris & Phillips, Ltd, 2002), 314. The biblical references noted are among many found throughout Sacred Scripture.

before David captured it and made it his capital in about 1000 BCE."[71]

In 1892, archaeologist Frederick J. Bliss discovered the first cuneiform tablet found in Palestine. This tablet was similar to the cuneiform tablets found at Tell el-Amarna in Egypt.[72] The discovery included thirty-five hundred-year-old clay tablets that were written in cuneiform during the fourteenth century BCE. The Sumerians probably developed the system of cuneiform writing before the last centuries of the fourth millennium BCE.[73] Cuneiform writing involved the use of a stylus to impress wedges into soft clay tablets. The tablets were then baked. The Semitic Sumerians devised cuneiform for themselves. However, it was quickly adopted by their successors and by various Indo-European groups scattered from India to Western Europe.[74]

Figure 4. **Left:** An early world map, circa 600 BCE, shows Babylon as a rectangle intersected by two vertical lines representing the Euphrates River. The small circle stands for surrounding kingdoms, and an ocean encircles the world. **Center:** A Babylonian tablet, circa 87 BCE, reports the arrival of the comet known as Halley. **Right:** Inscribed clay tablets

---

[71] Shanks, *Jerusalem: An Archaeological Biography*, 1.

[72] Thomas E. Levy, "Archaeology and the Bible," *EDB*, 91.

[73] "Cuneiform," in *The Columbia Encyclopedia*, 6th ed. (New York: Columbia University Press, 2001–2007). Http://www.bartleby.com/65/.

[74] Tenney and Packer, *Illustrated Manners and Customs*, 95.

from the ancient city of Ugarit, circa 1300 BCE. These tablets are the most important source of information we have about ancient Canaanite culture. They played an enormous role in understanding ancient Israelite religion.[75]

The tablets discovered in Tell el-Amarna included diplomatic letters written in Akkadian cuneiform characters. Akkadian cuneiform was the diplomatic language of international diplomacy in the fourteenth century BCE and provides much information about the local language.[76] All serious scholars who have examined the Tell el-Amarna letters agree that the name *"Urusalem"* mentioned in the letters clearly refers to Jerusalem. The six letters from the prince of *Urusalem*, Abdi Khiba [sic], to Pharaoh evidence that Jerusalem existed as a city during this critical historical period.[77] Although these are the earliest literary references to Jerusalem, archaeologists take us back to the Middle Bronze Age (2100–1600 BCE) when Jerusalem is referred to as *Rushalimum* in Egyptian execration texts preserved as hieroglyphics. Execration texts are those that curse, denounce, damn, or anathematize.[78]

In the early 1960s, British archaeologist Kathleen Kenyon located part of the earliest wall that enclosed Jeru-

---

[75] Todd Bolen/BiblePlaces.com, Babylonian map of the world from Sippar, 700–500 BCE, adr090506725; Babylonian observation of Halley's comet, 164 BCE, tb112004179; Judicial text with dynastic seal, 14th c, Ugarit, tb060408305dxo.

[76] Tenney and Packer, *Illustrated Manners and Customs*, 95.

[77] Alan Graeme Auld and Margreet Laura Steiner, *Jerusalem, Volume 1: From the Bronze Age to the Maccabees* (Macon, GA: Mercer University Press, 1996), 29.

[78] See Lester L. Grabbe, "Ethnic Groups in Jerusalem," in *Jerusalem in Ancient History and Tradition*, ed. Thomas L. Thompson (New York: Continuum International Publishing Group, 2004) 145–146. Crabbe identifies the prince as Abdi Heba and the Pharoah as Amenophis IV (Akhenaton). *Webster's New Collegiate Dictionary*, 1977, s.v. "Excration," 400.

salem. On the basis of some pottery shards that she found, she dated the wall to the Middle Bronze Age, approximately 1800 BCE.[79] In Psalm 48:2–3, Jerusalem is referred to as "the holy mountain, fairest of heights, the joy of all the earth." David's master stroke of genius was to name *Jebus* as the capital. By his capture of the city, he made *Jebus* a "royal city." The transfer of the Ark of the Covenant established the religious importance of the city. This importance was never lost.[80] Jerusalem is celebrated in the Psalms as the "city of God" (Ps. 46:5) and in Isaiah's famous vision when the Lord was returning to "Zion" (cf. Isa. 52:7–8). Jerusalem is set off by valleys on three sides. There is a sharp decline on the east into the Kidron Valley (traditionally identified as the Valley of Jehoshaphat). This valley separates Jerusalem from the higher Mount of Olives. The Valley of Hinnom is on the southwest of Jerusalem. The valley swings around the southern end of the mount to meet the Kidron Valley in the southeast at a place called *Haceldama* (meaning "field of blood"). The Hinnom Valley acquired an unpleasant reputation because it was used for the burning of garbage and the worship of pagan gods. The mount is split into two hills on the west and east by a shallower valley that is scarcely visible today. This valley was called the "Tyropoeon" or "Cheesemakers' Valley." The *Jebusite* city that fell to David was on the southern end of the east hill where the Kidron Valley and the Tyropoeon Valley join at a point to meet the Valley of Hinnom.[81]

Jerusalem has a history of being under siege. It had been taken five times and completely destroyed twice. Shishak, the king of Egypt, Antiochus, Pompey, Sosius, and Herod all took possession of Jerusalem. However, they preserved the city. The Babylonians demolished the city in 586/587 BCE,

---

[79] Shanks, *Jerusalem: An Archaeological Biography*, 1.
[80] Murphy, "A History of Israel," in *NJBC*, #75, §83, 1231–32.
[81] Brown, "Biblical Geography" in *NJBC*, #73, §92, 1190, 1192.

"four hundred and seventy-seven years and six months after David ruled."[82] Herod the Great ruled Judea from 37 to 4 BCE and is recognized as one of the great builders of all time. In a single generation, Herod built Jerusalem into one of the most magnificent capitals in the world. Among his many building projects, he doubled the size of the Temple Mount and completely rebuilt the Temple.[83] Josephus tells us,

> Now the outward face of the Temple in its front wanted nothing that was likely to surprise either men's minds or their eyes; for it was covered all over with plates of gold of great weight, and, at the first rising of the sun, reflected back a very fiery splendor, and made those who forced themselves to look upon it to turn their eyes away, just as they would have done at the sun's own rays. But this temple appeared to strangers, when they were coming to it at a distance, like a mountain covered with snow; for to those parts of it that were not gilt, they were exceedingly white.[84]

It is no wonder that Jesus was "moved to tears" as He looked over the city. In His humanity, He could appreciate the beauty and the history that was Jerusalem. In His divinity, He could foresee the year 70 CE when the city would be completely destroyed, its people ruthlessly murdered, and "not one stone left upon another stone." We turn again to Josephus for a detailed explanation of the destruction of Jerusalem. He states, "It was so thoroughly laid even with

---

[82] Whiston, *The New Complete Works of Josephus, Jewish War* 6.10.1.

[83] Shanks, *Jerusalem: An Archaeological Biography*, 137.

[84] Whiston, *The New Complete Works of Josephus, Jewish War* 5.5.6.

the ground by those that dug it up to the foundation, that there was left nothing to make those that came there believe it had ever been inhabited."[85]

When Jesus travelled to Jerusalem, He most likely approached Jerusalem from the east by travelling down the Jordan Valley. Almost everyone travelling from Galilee to Jerusalem would inevitably pass through Jericho, the chief oasis and place for rest and refreshment.[86] His last journey must have been bittersweet as He approached what He called "the city of the Great King" (cf. Matt. 5:34:35). This was the city where God was truly King.

Jesus was very familiar with Jerusalem. Because the Torah commanded that every Jew appear "three times a year before the Lord *and at a place he will choose*," Jesus and His parents made the difficult trip each year for the Feast of Passover (Luke 2:40). From the time He was a young boy, the Holy Family took Jesus to Jerusalem at the time of the Pasch. He was raised in a devoutly religious family.[87] His parents strictly followed Jewish customs and traditions. Every aspect of His life was steeped in Jewish culture, and His parents were His first teachers.[88] Jesus knew the importance of both the Temple and the city of Jerusalem. Who would have guessed that hidden in this royal city, this city of God, would be the road we would come to know as the Via Dolorosa? Who could have imagined that the people of this "holy mountain," this "joy of all the earth," would turn on the Son of God? Who would have believed that His beautiful Jerusalem would house the street that we would call the "Way of Sorrows"?

---

[85] Ibid. *Jewish War* 7.1.1.

[86] Walker, *In the Steps of Jesus*, 101.

[87] Pixner, *With Jesus in Jerusalem*, 83.

[88] Webster Patterson, *Sacred Sites* (Mahwah, NJ: Paulist Press, 2004), 121.

CHAPTER 5

THE GARDEN OF GETHSEMANE

I am troubled now. Yet what should I say? — 'Father save me from this hour?' But it was for this purpose that I came to this hour. (John 12:27)

The account of the Passion and death of Jesus begins in the Garden of Gethsemane where Jesus went to pray after supper with His disciples in the upper room. It is in the Garden of Gethsemane that He asked His Father to take the cup from Him. In that same garden, He accepted his Father's will and was arrested after being kissed by Judas (Luke 22:42; Mark 14:36). "The scene in the garden is only an introduction to the Passion, properly so called; for the Passion only begins with the arrest of Jesus. The introduction is designed as a theological setting for the whole story that follows."[89] The Mount of Olives was a familiar place for Jesus, and as the Bible implies, it was a favorite place for Him to seek rest and solitude. Scripture tells us "Each went to his own home, but Jesus went to the Mount of Olives (John 8:53)." Luke is

---

[89] De La Potterie, SJ, *The Hour of Jesus*, 40.

even more specific. He writes, "During the day, Jesus was teaching in the Temple area, but at night He would leave and stay at a place called the Mount of Olives (Luke 21:37)."

The Mount of Olives is so named because of the many olive trees that grew on it in ancient times. The height of the mountain affords a commanding view of Jerusalem. Bethany lies on the eastern portion of the mountain and is where Jesus raised His friend Lazarus from the dead. The grotto where He taught His disciples the principles of the faith lies at the summit. Gethsemane lies at the western foot of the slope. Christians revere the Mount of Olives as an extremely important holy site.[90]

Figure 5. A map of the area of Jerusalem in the first century CE.[91]

---

[90] Salomon and Milner, *Jesus 2000*, 189.

[91] Michael L. Russo. Photographed by Michael James Russo, April 25, 2012.

The Garden Of Gethsemane

Gethsemane means "oil press," and that is where the garden got its name, *Gat-Sh'manim*.[92] The process for making olive oil involved gathering baskets of olives and taking them to a shallow stone cistern. The olives were then crushed with a large millstone. Gethsemane was a comfortable and familiar place for Jesus. He and His disciples must have covered every path during His ministry.[93] However, there is no mention of a Garden of Gethsemane before the twelfth century. Both Matthew and Mark refer to Gethsemane as a place (Matt. 26:36; Mark 14:32). John makes reference to a garden but does not give it a name (John 18:1).

Figure 6. The Garden of Gethsemane.[94]

---

[92] Pixner, *With Jesus in Jerusalem*, 99.

[93] Leith Anderson, *Jesus: An Intimate Portrait of the Man, His Land, and His People* (Minneapolis, MN: Bethany House, 2005), 312.

[94] Michael L. Russo. Photographed by Michael James Russo, April 22, 2012.

The Via Dolorosa

Archaeologist Joan Taylor argues that "it would be extremely improbable that Jesus and His apostles would have spent the night out in the open sleeping amid the olive trees" and suggests that a cave would have been the ideal protection from inclement weather.[95] The Passion occurred in the spring, just before Passover, and the night air would have been cold and damp. Therefore, it is logical that they would have sought shelter in a cave.

Figure 7. The cave in the Garden of Gethsemane.[96]

---

[95] Joan E. Taylor is Honorary Research Fellow in the Department of History at University College London and Honorary Fellow in the Department of Religious Studies and Philosophy at Waikato University, Hamilton, New Zealand, and Honorary Research Fellow in the departments of Hebrew and Jewish Studies as well as History at UCL. Her book *Christians and the Holy Places: The Myth of Jewish Christian Origins* (1993) won an Irene Levi-Sala Prize in 1995. Dr. Irene Levi-Sala was a dedicated archaeologist who maintained a keen interest in the culture and archaeology of Israel and supported numerous scholarly enterprises in Israel. The purpose of the Irene Levi-Sala book prize is to encourage and reward high-quality publications on the archaeology of Israel. See Joan E. Taylor, Oxford University Press. http://www.oup.com/us/catalog /general/subject/ReligionTheology/Judaism /~~/ dmlldz11c2EmY2k9 OTc4M DE5OTI5MTQxMA==. Also see [ANE] Irene Levi-Sala Book Prize 2004. http://listhost.uchicago.edu/pipermail/ane/2004-April/013184.html.

[96] Todd Bolen/BiblePlaces.com, Garden of Gethsemane cave, tb012603209; Gethsemane cave2, tb012603838.

Remnants of an oil press were found in a cave. Taylor believes this is the place where Jesus was arrested. Today, the cave is considered one of the authentic sites related to Jesus's ministry in Jerusalem.[97] Bargil Pixner also speaks of a cave that was at the foot of the Mount of Olives. He suggests that eight of the apostles remained in the cave while Jesus went off to pray along with Peter, James, and John.[98] Scripture supports the statement that it was cold on the night Jesus was arrested (John 18:18). It is important to note that no one knows the exact spot where Jesus prayed and was eventually arrested. Because the area is near the ancient road leading from the Temple to the summit of the Mount of Olives, it is considered the most likely area.[99] Franciscan architect Antonio Barluzzi built a church commemorating the agony Jesus suffered in Gethsemane. The church is named the Church of All Nations. Funds from twelve different countries were used to build the church. The church was constructed between 1919 and 1924 and is also called the Church of the Agony. It symbolizes the place where Jesus was "overwhelmed with sorrow to the point of death."[100]

Prayer was central to Jesus's life and relationship to the Father. We read throughout Sacred Scripture that Jesus

---

[97] Taylor provides a detailed description of the cave and believes that Jesus was arrested inside or just outside the cave. However, the Gospels are not specific on this point. Joan E. Taylor, *Twenty-Four Hours That Changed the World Forever: An Easter Discussion*, Biblical Archaeology Review. http://www.bib-arch.org/online-exclusives/easter-03.asp. Shanks, *Jerusalem: An Archaeological Biography*, 186.

[98] Pixner, *With Jesus in Jerusalem*, 99. Pixner describes a cave on the southern side of the olive grove and states that Jesus was arrested when He returned to the cave "Where the other eight were staying."

[99] Patterson, *Sacred Sites*, 44; Sacred Destinations, "The Church of All Nations (Basilica of the Agony, Jerusalem)." http://www.sacred-destinations.com/israel/jerusalem-church-of-all-nations.htm.

[100] Salomon and Milner, *Jesus 2000*, 191.

would go off alone to pray. This night would have been no different. Although Peter, James, and John would accompany Him into the garden, He would then leave them and go off on His own to pray. Father Pixner provides an emotional image for us when he states, "In the moonlight, the three observed how cold perspiration suddenly broke out on His brow. There was trembling in His words (cf. Mark 14:35–36). Human nature and divine will were competing."[101]

Jesus prayed in anguish as the obedient Son of God, struggling to accept God's will. Scripture portrays the disciples as unaware of what was transpiring because they were sleeping each time Jesus returned to them.[102] Although He told the three disciples, "My soul is very sorrowful, even unto death" (Mark 14:34), they did not realize the impact of the events that were unfolding. Jesus prayed earnestly, and Luke 22:44 tells us, "He was in such agony and He prayed so fervently that His sweat became like drops of blood." This statement has caused much discussion among theologians for centuries. According to some forensic experts, Luke was not speaking figuratively or allegorically. The condition that the "doctor" Luke is describing is also identified in *Stedman's Medical Dictionary*.[103] The condition known as *hematidrosis* is defined as an excretion of blood or blood pigments in the sweat. Aristotle observed this condition in his time, and it was also referred to in *Hobart's Medical Language of St. Luke*.[104] Hematidrosis is associated with a

---

[101] Pixner, *With Jesus in Jerusalem*, 99.

[102] Daniel J. Harrington, SJ, "The Gospel According to Mark," in *NJBC*, #41, §98, 626.

[103] Drugs.com, *Stedman's Medical Dictionary*, s.v. "Hematridosis." http://www.drugs.com/dict/hematidrosis.html.

[104] Frederick T. Zugibe, MD, PhD, *The Crucifixion of Jesus: A Forensic Inquiry* (New York, NY: M. Evans and Company, 2005), 8. Dr. Zugibe disputes the findings of Pierre Barbet's book *A Doctor at Calvary* (Fort Collins, CO: Roman Catholic Books, 1953) citing the differences in experiment protocol and technology. Various other books

severe anxiety reaction triggered by fear. Dr. Frederick Zugibe, who conducted extensive research for his book *The Crucifixion of Jesus: A Forensic Inquiry*, identifies the fear center of the brain (identified as the *amygdala*). He explains that when the fear center is alerted, it sends out a defense alarm to the major brain centers. They in turn relay the alarm to the various body structures that trigger sweating, chest tightness, palpitations, acute anxiety, panic attacks, et cetera. Zugibe calls the defense system that is triggered by the fear center of the brain the fight-or-flight reaction. He suggests that in Gethsemane, Jesus's extreme fear, sadness, and anxiety initiated the fight-or flight reaction. He supports his opinion as follows:

> Jesus mission was clear, and He was able to envision the entire gamut of His suffering and death to come. This prelude produced extreme fear and satisfied all the medical criteria for initiating the symptomatic autonomic response. Jesus' heart pounded against His chest, a cold sweat appeared on His now pale skin, His pupils became dilated, His muscles tightened, and He began to tremble throughout the night.

---

and films explain this phenomenon. See *How Jesus Died: The Final 18 Hours*, dir. John Dauer, 35 min., (Trinity Pictures, 1994); *The Crucifixion of Christ, Return to the Cross*, dir. Mark E. Seremet, 180 min., (Bema Publishing, 2004); *Crucifixion*, 100 min., (New Video, 2008) for additional studies and commentary. Although each resource identifies slight discrepancies, a clear picture of the events of Christ's Passion and death emerges with minimal differences. Rev. William Kirk Hobart, LL.D., *The Medical Language of St. Luke: A Proof from Internal Evidence That "The Gospel According to St. Luke" and "The Acts of the Apostles" Were Written by the Same Person and That the Writer Was a Medical Man*, (Dublin: Hodges, Figgis and Company, 1882), 80–83. http://books.google.com/books?hl=en&id=jctJAAAAMAAJ&dq=Hobart's+medical+Language+of+St+Luke&printsec=frontcover&source=web&ots=rKCS8OXc6T&sig=FPFLTRo6f2z3mAveeDjt0sCuJOc-&sa=X&oi=book_result&resnum=1&ct=result # PPP3,M1.

Therefore, to sum it up in a nutshell, the most logical explanation for the *hematidrosis* is as follows. The severe mental anxiety due to a profound fear of His prescient sufferings stimulated the fear center of the brain (*amygdala*), which sent out a general alarm to all centers of the brain, invoking a full-scale fight-or-flight reaction. This reaction lasted for hours, resulting in a state of total exhaustion, only to end abruptly with a severe counter reaction after the angel ministered to Him and He accepted His fate. This caused severe dilation and rupture of the blood vessels into the sweat glands, causing hemorrhage into the ducts of the sweat glands and the subsequent extrusion out onto the skin, exactly as Luke described it.[105]

In the garden we see Jesus praying alone. In His agony, His mission is fully revealed to Him, and He cries out to the Father in anguish. In His humanity, He was praying for another solution. In His divinity, He would accept the Father's will.

A key point to learn from Gethsemane is that Jesus actively chose the path to the cross. He knew the garden paths so well that He could have easily escaped and been in Bethany within forty minutes.[106] Instead of fleeing by some obscure path, Jesus waited for His betrayer and the band of soldiers that would take Him away. Although there is no direct response from God to Jesus's prayer for deliverance, ultimately Jesus rises resolved to encounter the betrayer, leaving us to assume that He has understood God's answer to be that he must drink the cup and face the hour that is at hand.[107] However, Jesus's prayer to His Father does

---

[105] Zugibe, *The Crucifixion of Jesus*, 11–14. See *How Jesus Died: The Final 18 Hours*, dir. John Dauer; *The Crucifixion of Christ, Return to the Cross*, dir. Mark E. Seremet; *Crucifixion*, 100 min.

[106] Walker, *In the Steps of Jesus*, 123.

[107] Raymond E. Brown, SS, *A Crucified Christ in Holy Week* (Collegeville, MN: The Liturgical Press, 1986), 22.

not remain unanswered. God sends an angel to strengthen Him. This divine assistance brings Jesus to *agonia,* a Greek term that does not refer to agony in the ordinary sense but describes the supreme tension of the athlete covered with sweat at the start of the contest. In that spirit, Jesus rises from His prayer ready to enter the trial.[108]

Jesus knew the importance of completing His mission, and He was in control. Just as in the first garden there was a meeting between Adam and the serpent (the symbol of the devil), in the second garden there is a meeting between the second Adam, Jesus, and the representatives of Satan, Judas and his companions.[109] Judas, one of the twelve, one of those handpicked by Jesus, would turn against his friend. Judas had become the personification of darkness because Satan had entered him (Luke 22:3; John 13:2).[110]

---

[108] Ibid., 50.

[109] De La Potterie, SJ, *The Hour of Jesus,* 31.

[110] Ibid., 29. De La Potterie's states, "For the author of the Fourth Gospel, Judas had become the personification of the powers of darkness precisely because Satan had entered him."

CHAPTER 6

THE STATIONS OF THE CROSS

But He was pierced for our offenses, crushed for our sins, upon Him was the chastisement that makes us whole, by His stripes we were healed. We had all gone astray like sheep, each following his own way; but the Lord laid upon Him the guilt of us all. Though He was harshly treated, He submitted and opened not His mouth; like a lamb led to the slaughter or a sheep before the shearers, He was silent and opened not His mouth. (Isaiah 53:5–7)

The Stations of the Cross, a series of meditations focusing on the Passion and death of Jesus Christ, have been one of the most popular devotions embraced by Christians worldwide.[111] As noted in chapter 1, the term "Stations" was first used by an English pilgrim, William Wey, who visited Jerusalem in 1458 and again in 1462.[112] Those who

---

[111] Richard Holloway, *A Death in Jerusalem* (London: Faith Press, 1986), 1.

[112] Macpherson, *Pilgrim Preacher,* 32. Macpherson is quoting from M. Walsh, *A Dictionary of Devotions* (London: Burns Oates, 1993), 251.

choose to meditate on Christ's Passion and death through the Stations of the Cross find that the Passion is still living and active—still sacramentally present to them. For them, this is not just an event in the past or a piece of history. For these devoted followers of Christ, the Stations of the Cross are more than just works of art on the walls of churches; they can be revelatory symbols, the means through which God communicates His divine truth to men and women.[113] For those who believe, those who enter into the mystery of Christ's salvific work, the remembrance of the Passion and death of Christ is a way of actualizing and making it present now. To the outsider or the occasional participant, this may not appear to be the case. The reason for this is because the meaning of the devotional experience cannot first be found by treating it merely as an historical event. The spiritual meaning always lies within. We must come to the cross with an open mind and heart and submit ourselves to God's will, just as Jesus obediently accepted the will of the Father.[114]

> In the Stations of the Cross the person who has the eye of faith sees the story of Christ's historical Passion—His own individual story—and the story of the suffering world, in which Christ's Passion goes on through time; the Way of the Cross, which, though it leads to the tomb and the dark sleep of death, leads on beyond it to the waking morning of resurrection and the everlasting springtime of life.[115]

The purpose of the Stations of the Cross is to provide the faithful with the opportunity to make, in spirit, a pilgrimage to the chief sites in the Holy Land that memorialize Christ's

---

[113] Holloway, *A Death in Jerusalem*, 4.

[114] Ibid., 3.

[115] Caryll Houselander, *The Way of the Cross* (Liguori, MO: Liguori Publications, 2002), xi.

sufferings and death. This devotion has particularly been embraced by Catholics and become one of their most popular devotions. The devotion is carried out by passing from Station to Station, reciting specific prayers and meditating on the individual events from Jesus's condemnation to the placing of Jesus in the tomb. There are variations of the Stations of the Cross that include a closing dedicated to the Resurrection of Christ. The closing is omitted when praying the Stations of the Cross on Good Friday.[116] The practice of the devotion constitutes a miniature pilgrimage to the holy places in Jerusalem.[117] Father Balthasar Alvarez, spiritual director to St. Theresa of Avila, said, "Ignorance of the treasures that we possess in Jesus was the ruin of Christians."[118] Therefore, his most favorite meditation was on the Passion of Christ. St. Bonaventure advises, "He who desires to go on advancing from virtue to virtue, from grace to grace, should meditate continually on the Passion of Jesus." He adds, "There is no practice more profitable for the entire sanctification of the soul than frequent meditation on the sufferings of Christ." According to St. Alphonsus de Liguori, St. Augustine is to have said that "A single tear shed at the remembrance of the Passion of Jesus is worth more than a pilgrimage to Jerusalem, or a year of fasting on bread and water."[119]

During the fifteenth and sixteenth centuries, several reproductions of the holy places were set up in different locations throughout Europe. Upon his return from the Holy Land, the Blessed Alvarez (d. 1420) built a series of chapels at the Dominican Friary of Cordova in which the prin-

---

[116] *The Way of the Cross* (Baltimore, MD: Barton-Cotton, Inc., 1965).

[117] Alston, "Way of the Cross."

[118] St. Alphonsus De Liguori, *The Passion and the Death of Jesus Christ* (Brooklyn, NY: Redemptorist Fathers, 1927), 19.

[119] Ibid., 20.

cipal scenes of the Passion were painted. Blessed Eustochia, a poor Clare, constructed a similar set of Stations near her convent in Messina at around the same time. Stations were erected in Görlitz by G. Emmerich in 1465 and in Nüremburg by Ketzel in 1468 as well as in many other locations by many other persons devoted to the remembrance of the Passion and death of Jesus.[120] The Stations of the Cross became one of the most enduring expressions of devotion to the Passion of Jesus.

The number of Stations varied at times, but William Wey does provide a list of fourteen Stations. However, only five correspond with Stations that we identify today. Seven are remotely connected to the Via Dolorosa. The list of the Stations provided by William Wey includes the *House of Dives*[121], *The City Gate through Which Christ Passed*, *The Probatic Pool*,[122] *The Ecce Homo Arch*, the *Blessed Virgin's*

---

[120] Alston, "Way of the Cross."

[121] The word "Dives" is not used in the Bible as a proper noun. However, in the Middle Ages, it was used to identify the name of the rich man in the parable of the rich man and Lazarus, Luke 16:19–31. The "House of Dives" is still pointed out in Jerusalem; but if the house ever existed, it has long since disappeared. Wendell Reilly, "Dives" in *The Catholic Encyclopedia*, vol 5, (New York: Robert Appleton Company, 1912). http://www.newadvent.org /cathen /05048a.htm. According to Todd Bolen and David Bivin, the houses of Dives and Lazarus are located at the fourth and fifth Stations. The fourth Station (the house of Lazarus) is where Jesus is said to have met His mother along the route to Calvary. The fifth Station is where Simon of Cyrene helps Jesus carry the cross. The house of Dives is said to be located at the fifth Station. See David Bivin, "Historic Views of the Holy Land," *Views That Have Vanished: The Photographs of David Bivin*, CD, 2008.

[122] The Probatic Pool is called "Bethsaida" in Hebrew and is also known as "Bethesda" and "Bethsaida." Walter Elliott, *The Life of Jesus Christ: Embracing the Entire Gospel* (New York: The Catholic Book Exchange, 1908), 257. This is the pool where the paralytic was healed as told in John 5:2–9.

School, and *The Houses of Herod and Simon the Pharisee*. Adrichomius wrote a book titled *Jerusalem sicut Christi tempore floruit*, which was published in 1584. In the book, Adrichomius identified twelve Stations that correspond exactly with the first twelve Stations that we have today.

During the sixteenth century, many devotional manuals containing prayers to be used for the Stations were distributed throughout Europe for the benefit of those who could not visit the Holy Land. When pilgrim Roman Boffin traveled to Jerusalem in 1515 to obtain concrete details, two friars told him that there should be thirty-one Stations. Various other manuals of the time identified nineteen, twenty-five, and thirty-seven Stations. Another pilgrim, Zuallardo, who wrote a devotional book in 1587, provided a full series of prayers for the shrines of the Holy Sepulchre, which were under the care of the Franciscans. However, he excluded any prayers for the Stations located inside the Church of the Holy Sepulchre. He explained his reason: "It is not permitted to make any halt, nor to pay veneration to them with uncovered head, not to make any other demonstration." This may be due to the Turkish domination at that time.[123] The political situation under the Turks did not allow the pilgrims to openly pray. However, in 1731, Pope Clement XII issued a decree that confirmed the validity of the Stations of the Cross and fixed the number as we have it today.[124] In 1741, Pope Benedict XIV reconfirmed Clement XII's decree to erect Stations of the Cross in all churches and the indulgences attached to the devotion. Popularity for praying the Stations of the Cross quickly grew.[125]

---

[123] Alston, "Way of the Cross."

[124] Hela Crown-Tamir, *How to Walk in the Footsteps of Jesus and the Prophets* (Jerusalem: Gefen Publishing House LTD, 2000), 183.

[125] Martin Bialas, CP, *The Mysticism of the Passion of St. Paul of the Cross* (San Francisco, CA: Ignatius Press, 1990), 96.

The Stations Of The Cross

One may deduce from historical information that our present devotion comes from the efforts established in different parts of Europe, and not from Jerusalem. The sixteenth-century devotional writers were more responsible for the creation of the devotions than the practice of pilgrims traveling to the holy places.

For those who did get to the Holy Land, the Franciscans were there to cater for their needs by providing hospices and by caring for existing shrines, "discovering" new ones, and by maintaining liturgical functions at these sites. In the 15th century, for example, the friars set up, and thus made possible, preaching of "Stations of the Cross" on the route supposedly taken by Jesus on the way to Calvary.[126]

Additions and omissions seem to confirm that our current Stations are derived from pious manuals of devotion rather than from Jerusalem itself.[127] Our current Stations include Jesus being condemned, carrying His cross, falling three times, meeting His mother, getting help from Simon of Cyrene, having His face wiped by Veronica, meeting the women of Jerusalem, being stripped of His clothes, being nailed to the Cross, dying on the cross, Jesus's body being taken from the cross, and the placement of His body in the tomb.[128] In 1799, the diocese of Vienna created a special set of eleven Stations that included the Agony in the Garden, the Betrayal by Judas, the Scourging, the Crowning with Thorns, Jesus Condemned to Death, Christ Meeting Simon of Cyrene, the Women of Jerusalem, Jesus Tasting the Gall,

---

[126] Macpherson, *Pilgrim Preacher*, 32. Macpherson is quoting from M. Walsh, *A Dictionary of Devotions* (London: Burns Oates, 1993), 32.

[127] Ibid., 32.

[128] Alston, "Way of the Cross."

Jesus Being Nailed to the Cross, Jesus' Death on the Cross, and Jesus' Body Being Taken Down from the Cross.[129]

On Good Friday 1991, Pope John Paul II changed the format of the Stations of the Cross as he prayed them with a crowd of people at the Roman Colosseum. He kept some of the traditional Stations, dropped others, and inserted new ones. Pope John Paul II's version held true to the events as recorded in the Gospels. His Stations of the Cross include the Agony of Jesus in the Garden of Olives, The Betrayal and Arrest of Jesus, the Sanhedrin Condemns Jesus, Peter Denies Jesus, Pilate Condemns Jesus to the Cross, Jesus is Scourged and Crowned with Thorns, Jesus is Mocked by the Soldiers and Given His Cross, Simon the Cyrenean[sic] Helps Jesus to Carry His Cross, Jesus Meets the Women of Jerusalem, Jesus is Crucified, Jesus Promises Paradise to the Penitent Criminal, Jesus Speaks to His Mother and His Disciple, Jesus Dies on the Cross, The Burial of Jesus, and Jesus Rises from the Dead.[130]

Whatever devotion we choose, as we contemplate the Passion and death of Christ, we will learn much about human nature. More importantly, we will learn about God's way with human nature. Theologian Hans Urs von Balthasar reminds us of the interpretations of the cross in Paul and John: "The Son's Cross is the revelation of the Father's love (Romans 8, 32; John 3, 16), and the bloody outpouring of that love comes into its inner fulfillment in the shedding abroad of their common Spirit into the hearts of men (Romans 5:5)."[131]

---

[129] Ibid.

[130] Joseph M. Champlin, *The Stations of the Cross with Pope John Paul II* (Liguori, MO: Liguori Publications, 1994).

[131] Hans Urs von Balthasar, *Mysterium Paschale* (San Francisco, CA: Ignatius Press, 2000), 140.

CHAPTER 7

THE FIRST STATION: JESUS IS CONDEMNED TO DEATH

"Are you king of the Jews?" Jesus answered, "My kingdom does not belong to this world. If my kingdom did belong to this world, my attendants [would] be fighting to keep me from being handed over to the Jews. But as it is, my kingdom is not here. So Pilate said to Him, "Then you are a king?" Jesus answered, "You say I am a king. For this I was born and for this I came into the world, to testify to the truth." (John 18:33, 36–37)

𝓘n an attempt to comprehend Jesus's being condemned to death, we need to examine the case against Jesus. Jesus, an innocent man, is taken prisoner and dragged from His normally peaceful retreat on the Mount of Olives. When Jesus spoke to the crowds on the Mount of Olives, they admired His teaching (Matt. 7:28). When those sent to arrest Him by the chief priest and Pharisees returned empty handed, they replied, "Never before has anyone spoken like this one (John 7:46)." To make any sense out of the situation, one must examine

The Via Dolorosa

---

some of Jesus's statements that challenged the people. John the Baptist was revered by the people as a prophet of God, a holy man. In Matthew 11:10, Jesus told the crowds that He was greater than John. The people considered Jonah to be a great prophet and preacher of repentance. In Matthew 12:41, Jesus told the people, "There is something greater than Jonah here." In the same discourse, Jesus added, "There is something greater than Solomon here" (cf. Matt. 12:41–42). One can only imagine the reaction to such a statement—"Someone greater than Solomon," a man gifted by God with great wisdom!

Jesus continued to challenge the minds and hearts of the people. Moses was their greatest prophet and lawgiver. However, Jesus made it clear that it was He, Jesus, who had come to fulfill the law (Matt. 5:17). If that was not shocking enough, Jesus addressed His relationship with Abraham clearly when He stated, "Amen, amen, I say to you, before Abraham came to be, I AM (John 8:58)." At this, the people tried to stone Jesus, but He was able to escape. Threats against His life did not deter Jesus from speaking out. He went on to tell the people that He was greater than the Temple (Matt. 12:6) and that He was Lord of the Sabbath (Matt. 12:8). Jesus even claimed that the angels were subordinate to Him when He stated, "For the Son of Man will come with His angels in His Father's glory and then He will repay everyone according to his conduct." (Matt. 16:27). G. Rooney points out: "The one thing they burned to hear from Him, yet He showed reluctance in telling them—was that He was the Messiah."[132] People were amazed at the authority with which Jesus spoke. Jesus spoke the truth with conviction. The words He spoke were from God, and He wanted everyone to believe and follow His teachings.[133] Jesus did not hide the fact that He came from God and was sent by God (John 8:42).

---

[132] Gerard Rooney, CP, *The Mystery of Calvary* (New York, NY: Macmillan Company, 1959), 2-3.

[133] Anderson, *Jesus*, 85.

The First Station: Jesus Is Condemned To Death

Chapter 53 of Isaiah reads like an eyewitness account of Jesus's Passion and death. "Jesus wove together the prophecies of Daniel and Isaiah and rightly applied them to Himself.[134]" For the most part, Jesus remained silent at His trial. He knew the Law. He knew that it was up to the accusers to prove their case. If witnesses were found guilty of perjury, they would have been given the same punishment as the original defendant if the defendant had been found guilty. Jesus knew that He was not required to answer.[135] The burden of proof was clearly on the accusers and not on the defendant. The rules for trial according to the Talmud state:

> Anyone accused of a capital offense was legally protected from self-incrimination and could not be asked questions in his trial. Witnesses were required to give complete testimony. Unlike modern western judicial systems where the testimony of one witness may build on the testimony of another witness, the Jewish witness had to give his complete testimony of the whole crime. Those who testified were to be eyewitnesses and had to corroborate that any [sic] other witness had also seen the crime.[136]

---

[134] Rooney, *The Mystery of Calvary*, 7.

[135] Anderson, *Jesus*, 321.

[136] Ibid., 318. See *Babylonian Talmud, Book 9: Tracts Maccoth, Shebuoth, Eduyoth, Abuda Zara, and Horioth,* tr. By Michael L. Rodkinson, 1918. http://sacred-texts.com. Chapter one of *Tract Maccoth* deals with the issue of punishment for giving false witness. The Talmud supports its position in Scripture. Deut. 19:15–19 states, "One witness alone shall not take the stand against a man in regard to any crime or any offense of which he may be found guilty; a judicial act shall be established only on the testimony of two or three witnesses. If an unjust witness takes the stand against a man to accuse him of a defection from the law, the two parties in the dispute shall appear before the Lord in the presence of the priests or judges in office at that time; and if after a thorough investigation the judges find that the witness is a false witness and has accused his kinsman falsely, you shall do to him as he planned to do to his kinsman."

The Via Dolorosa

The entire process seems to have frustrated and angered Caiaphas. When Caiaphas asked Jesus whether He was the Messiah, the Son of God, Jesus replied, "You have said so" (Matt. 26:64). Caiaphas was careful in his choice of words. According to Scripture, Caiaphas ordered Jesus to respond "under oath." When questioned under oath, Jesus was bound under Jewish law to respond. He knew that His response would seal His fate. The legal accusation brought against Him was blasphemy.[137] R. Holloway points out, "Jesus was found guilty not because He spoke *about* God but *as* God. As the one sent from God."[138]

Jesus was placed in prison overnight so that the Sanhedrin could fulfill its responsibility of pondering the accusation and consequences before giving their final verdict. Because the Jewish leadership did not have the authority to put someone to death, it became the responsibility of the Romans to impose the death sentence. Therefore, the Sanhedrin had plenty of time overnight to prepare the necessary indictment to present to Pontius Pilate, the Roman procurator.[139]

The first Station of the Cross, in which the condemnation of Christ is memorialized, is today located in the courtyard of the Muslim Omariye College. The current building was constructed in the Mameluke period (1250–1517 CE) on the foundation of the Antonia Fortress. Today, there is no church or chapel on the exact spot to commemorate or identify this Station. However, during the Crusader period (1095–1291 CE) there was a chapel commemorating Jesus's being crowned with thorns. The chapel was destroyed in an earthquake that struck the area in 1927.[140] According to some

---

[137] Pixner, *With Jesus in Jerusalem*, 116.
[138] Holloway, *A Death in Jerusalem*, 12.
[139] Pixner, *With Jesus in Jerusalem*, 117–8.
[140] Salomon and Milner, *Jesus 2000*, 193.

The First Station: Jesus Is Condemned To Death

traditions, this is the place where Jesus was persecuted by Roman soldiers and condemned to death by Pontius Pilate.

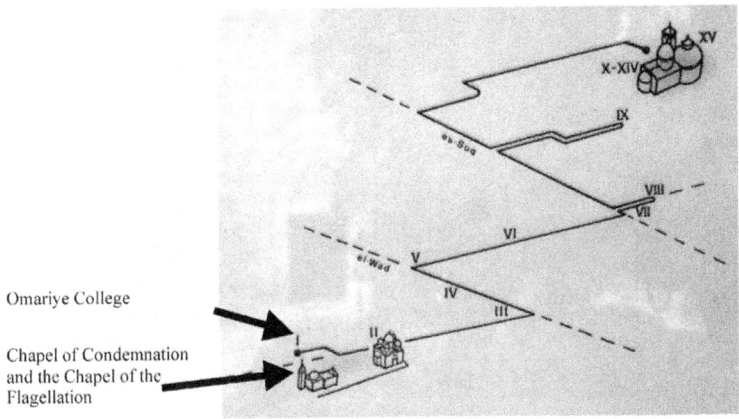

Figure 8. A street map showing the approximate location of the Muslim Omariye College and the Chapel of Condemnation. The Chapel of Flagellation marking where Jesus was scourged by the Roman soldiers is located next to the Chapel of Condemnation.[141]

The sanctuary of the *Chapel of Condemnation* marks the first Station of the Cross. The painting above the altar depicts Pilate washing his hands and Jesus approaching His cross. To the right of the painting is a papier-mâché statue of Jesus bearing His cross.

---

[141] Public domain.

The Via Dolorosa

Figure 9. The altar containing the painting of Pilate washing his hands. The paper maché statue is to the right of the altar.[142]

Brother Wendelin of Menden, a Franciscan architect, built the Chapel of Condemnation in 1903–1904. The floor of the chapel consists of large paving stones and extends to the Franciscan museum and the Convent of the Sisters of Zion. Some of the paving stones are etched with games.[143] The Roman soldiers played these games during slow periods on their watch. The "Stone Pavement" is identified with the Lithostrotos (also known as the judgment seat). This is the Stone Pavement (in Hebrew is called Gabbatha) that is mentioned in John 19:13.[144]

From the courtyard of the Omariye College, one can see two chapels, the Chapel of Condemnation and the Chapel of

---

[142] Michael L. Russo. Photographed by Michael James Russo, April 25, 2012.

[143] John Abela, OFM and Michael Olteau, "Jerusalem, The Way of the Cross, Via Crucis," at Franciscan Cyberspot-Christusrex 1998. http://www.christusrex.org/www1/jvc/TVCstatn02.html.

[144] Salomon and Milner, *Jesus 2000*, 193.

The First Station: Jesus Is Condemned To Death

the Flagellation. The Chapel of the Flagellation was originally built in the twelfth century CE. Pilgrims report that it was used as a refuse dump, a stable, and a weaver's shop. By 1838, it was in complete ruin when Ibrahim Pasha, conqueror of the Turks, gave the place to the Franciscans. Through the generosity of King Maximilian of Bavaria, the chapel was quickly rebuilt one year later. The Chapel of Flagellation underwent another complete restoration in 1927–1929 by architect Antonio Barluzzi. Barluzzi was born in Rome in 1884, and his family had served the Holy See for generations. He studied architecture in Rome and traveled to Jerusalem in 1911 to build a hospital for the Italian Missionary Society. He was devoted to the Holy Land, and as a Franciscan lay brother, he helped change the landscape of the Holy Land by building churches at Gethsemane, Mount Tabor, Jericho, and other holy sites.[145]

Jesus retained His calm demeanor as He stood in front of Pilate. In John, "The account of the passion is transformed into a victory march of Jesus to His enthronement on the cross. Jesus is calmly in charge of His trial, and it becomes clear that it is Pilate and the Jewish leaders who are actually on trial."[146] The Jewish leaders had Jesus arrested, bound, and brought before Pilate. They built their case against Him, but what was the real motive? The Jewish leaders were motivated by their desire to preserve their own power and position. It was important for them to maintain the religious status quo. They were blinded to the truth that was in the words and signs of Jesus. "They were 'blind' in the deepest spiritual sense of that word." They had progressively transformed the religion of *YHWH* into a commitment to the institution so that they

---

[145] Cohen, *Saving the Holy Sepulchre*, 67–68.

[146] Sandra M. Schneiders, *Written That You Might Believe: Encountering Jesus in the Fourth Gospel* (New York, NY: The Crossroad Publishing Company, 2003), 57.

could guarantee their own status and power. They abandoned their commitment to God.[147]

Both Mark and Matthew tell us that Pilate wanted to release Jesus because "He perceived that it was out of envy that the chief priests had handed Him over. (Matt. 15:10; Mark 27:18)." The Jewish leaders were concerned that if they did not take drastic action, the risk of Jesus convincing all to believe in Him would be too great and the Romans would take all of their land as well as their nation (John 11:48). Therefore, the priests not only plotted to have Jesus killed, they were able to use the state to do the job for them.[148]

Although Pilate thought Jesus was innocent, his own self-interest kept him from resisting the pressures placed upon him by the Jewish leaders. The crowds were too much for him, and the threat of an uprising was rapidly increasing. "Instead of doing what he knows is right, he weakly capitulates to their demands in order to maintain both public order and his own political neck."[149]

When his solution of suggesting that Jesus be released over the criminal Barabbas failed, Pilate released Barabbas to the mob and sent Jesus to be scourged. Scourging was the usual procedure prior to any crucifixion. Many people associate the word *scourging* with a mere beating using a whiplike object. In reality, flagellation or scourging was a brutal and inhumane punishment using an instrument called a *flagrum*. The most common form for the flagrum was a leather whip containing many leather tails with small metal balls or sheep bones attached to the end of each tail. The Romans had no laws governing a specific number of lashes. However, Mosaic Law stated that the lashes could not exceed forty. Usually, thirty-nine lashes were given to ensure compliance with Mosaic Law. In reality, the number of lashes

---

[147] Ibid., 86, 91.

[148] Holloway, *A Death in Jerusalem*, 16–17.

[149] Carter, *Pontius Pilate*, 5.

was determined by the executioners because they used this form of torture to satisfy their sadistic desires. During Caligula's reign (37–41 CE), Jews in Alexandria were tortured and crucified in the arena as entertainment.[150] M. Hengel tells us that the Romans would vary their methods of execution: "Crucifixion was a punishment in which the caprice and sadism of the executioners were given full reign." Any attempts to provide an archaeological description of crucifixion are in vain.[151] R. Martin concurs that crucifixion was uncivilized and involved unimaginable pain and unmerciful humiliation.[152] The number of lashes also depended on who the condemned person was and the seriousness of the crime. The Romans did not want the victim to succumb too quickly, but the beating was severe enough to bring the prisoner to the brink of death.[153] The leather thongs cut the skin, and the metal balls and small bones (called *tali*) dug deep into the flesh. There was a great deal of blood loss, which lowered the resistance of the victim. Scourging was an ancient custom used under Alexander and Antiochus Epiphanes. It was also used in

---

[150] *EDB*, 200 ed., s.v. "Crucifixion," 298; Gerald G. O'Collins, "Crucifixion," *ABD*, vol. 1, 1992 ed., 1207; Hengel, *Crucifixion*, 24–25, 35. Josephus reports, "So the soldiers, out of the wrath and hatred they bore the Jews, nailed those they caught, one after the other, to the crosses, by way of jest, when their multitude was so great, that room was wanting for the crosses, and crosses wanting for the bodies." Whiston, *Josephus, Jewish Wars*, 5.11.1, 874.

[151] Martin Hengel, *Crucifixion* (Philadelphia, PA: Fortress Press, 1977), 25; Dennis Gaertner, "Scourging," *EDB*, 1173. O'Collins discusses various examples of crucifixion in "Crucifixion," *ABD*, vol. 1, 1207-1210.

[152] Regis Martin, *Suffering of Love* (San Francisco, CA: Ignatius Press, 2006), 85; Donahue, "Crucifixion," *EDB*, 298. O'Collins, "Crucifixion," *ABD*, 1207–1210.

[153] Zugibe, *The Crucifixion of Jesus*, 19–20. See *How Jesus Died: The Final 18 Hours*, dir. John Dauer; *The Crucifixion of Christ, Return to the Cross*, dir. Mark E. Seremet; *Crucifixion*, 100 min.; O'Collins, "Crucifixion," *ABD*, vol. 1, 1209.

ancient Carthage.[154] The severity of the scourging depended on the disposition of the *lictors* and was intended to weaken the victim to a state just short of collapse or death.[155]

As the Roman soldiers repeatedly struck the victim's back with full force, the iron balls caused deep contusions, and the leather thongs and sheep bones cut deep into the skin and tissues. As the flogging continued, the lacerations would tear into the underlying skeletal muscles and produce quivering ribbons of bleeding flesh. Pain and blood loss generally set the stage for circulatory shock. The extent of blood loss may have been a determining factor in how long the victim was able to survive on the cross.

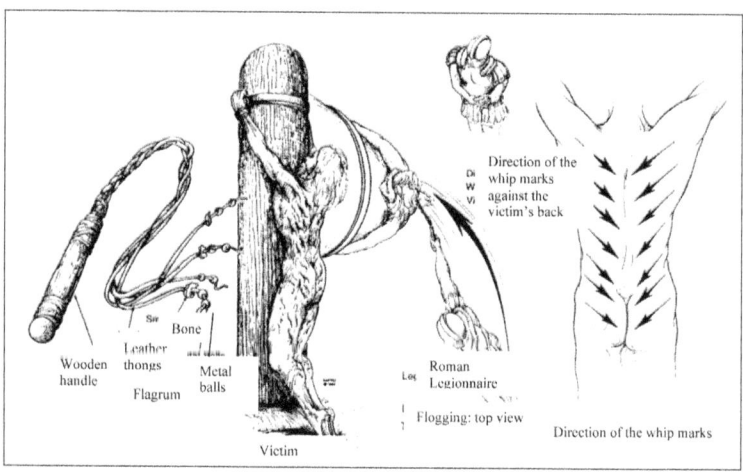

Figure 10. **Left:** A *flagrum* with lead balls and sheep bones tied into leather thongs. **Center left:** A naked victim tied to flogging post. **Center**

---

[154] Barbet, A *Doctor at Calvary*, 47–48. O'Collins, "Crucifixion," *ABD*, vol. 1, 1208–1209.

[155] *Webster's New Collegiate Dictionary* defines *Lictor* as a Roman officer who bears the fasces as the insignia of his office and whose duties include accompanying the magistrate. A *fasces* was a bundle of rods that included an ax. The *fasces* was a badge of authority.

right: View from above, showing the position of the *lictors.* **Right:** The direction of wounds inflicted by the *flagrum.*[156]

When the soldiers completed the scourging, they moved to the next phase of their madness. It was the custom to mock and demean the condemned person in every way imaginable.[157] Because Jesus was accused of making Himself the King of the Jews, the Romans did not have to think too hard about ways to mock and humiliate Him. Sacred Scripture tells us that the soldiers clothed Jesus in a purple robe and placed a reed in His right hand and a crown of thorns on His head (Matt. 27:29; Mark 15:17). According to Barbet, the crown was in the form of a hat. This meant that a large number of thorns were in contact with the entire top of Jesus's head, including the front, back, and sides. The blows to the face and head would have irritated the nerves of His face, lips, and head. The pain would have resembled that from an electric shock or being touched with a hot poker. Bleeding would have resulted from the thorns penetrating small blood vessels. The pain may have stopped abruptly at times only to return with full force. The slightest movement or breeze would have brought excruciating pain.[158] This is

---

[156] William D. Edwards, MD, Wesley J Gabel, MDiv, and Floyd E. Hosmer, MS, AMI, "The Physical Death of Jesus Christ," *Journal of the American Medical Association*, vol. 255 number 11. http://www.bibleanswer.com/x_death.htm. The article can also be found on http://www.frugalsites.net/jesus/welcome.htm. Also see Barbet, *A Doctor at Calvary*, 48, and Zugibe, *The Crucifixion of Jesus*, 20–21. J. Blinzler also presents a detailed explanation of the scourging. See J. Blinzler, *The Trial of Jesus* (Westminster MD: Newman, 1959) 226–26, 233–35. Dennis Gaertner, "Scourging," *EDB*, 2000, ed., s.v. 1173.

[157] Barbet, *A Doctor at Calvary*, 54; Martin, *Suffering of Love*, 85; Pixner, *With Jesus in Jerusalem*, 135. O'Collins, Crucifixion," *ABD*, vol. 1, 1209.

[158] Barbet, *A Doctor at Calvary*, 85; Zugibe, *The Crucifixion of Jesus*, 34; See *How Jesus Died: The Final 18 Hours*, dir. John Dauer; *The*

the state in which Pilate saw Jesus when He was returned to him after the scourging.

The traumatic shock from the brutal scourging would have been further enhanced by the paradoxical pains across the face. Exacerbations and remissions of throbbing bolts of pain would have occurred all the way to Calvary and during the crucifixion, activated by the movements of walking, falling, and twisting; from the pressure of the thorns against the cross; and from the many shoves and blows by the soldiers. Considering the plethora of blood vessels in the head and the effects of the crown of thorns, it is clear that the blood would have run freely down Jesus' face. The severe pains from the trigeminal neuralgia and, the multiple strikes to Jesus' head region and the crown of thorns, added to the trauma already received from the brutal scourging and beating at the home of Caiaphas thereby deepening the degree of traumatic shock. At this time, there would be significant fluid buildup around the lungs, which was slowly developing due to the severe beating to the chest during the flogging. At this stage, Jesus would be progressively weaker, light-headed, ashen in color, somewhat short of breath, and unsteady on His feet, and He would experience intermittent episodes of sweating.[159]

A monumental arch from the Roman period is thought to be a part of the Praetorium building. The arch is aptly named the Ecce Homo Arch. According to tradition, it is believed that this is the place where Pilate presented Jesus to the

---

Crucifixion of Christ, Return to the Cross, dir. Mark E. Seremet; *Crucifixion*, 100 min. Of the more than seventy species of thornlike plants growing in the Holy Land, two common thorns have been identified with the crown of thorns worn by Jesus: the *Ziziphus spina-christs* and the *Paliurus spina-christi*. However, it is impossible to discern which plant was actually used. Megan Bishop Moore, "Thorn," in *EBD*, 1304.

[159] Zugibe, *The Crucifixion of Jesus*, 36–37.

The First Station: Jesus Is Condemned To Death

crowd and said, "Ecce Homo," that is, "Behold the Man." The trial was conducted at the Stone Pavement (in Latin, the *Lithostrotos*) where Pilate sat on the judge's seat.[160]

Figure 11. **Left:** The Ecce Homo Arch as it is today. **Right:** The Stone Pavement (*Lithostrotos*) where Pilate sat on the judge's seat and condemned Jesus to death.[161]

Weighing his political options, it is from the Stone Pavement that Pilate sentenced Jesus to flogging and death by crucifixion. The flagstones identified with the *Lithostrotos* begin on the north side of the Antonia Tower and continue up to the Convent of the Sisters of Zion.[162]

According to F. Zugibe, the word "crucifixion" is derived from the Latin word *cruciare*, which means to torture and torment. It was reserved for traitors, slaves, hardened mur-

---

[160] Salomon, Milner, *Jesus 2000*, 193; David R. Beck, "Gabbatha," *EDB*, 474. A brief description of "The Pavement" can be found in *EDB*, 1021. Reference to the "Lithostroton" is also found in *EDB*, 817; John McRay, "Gabbatha," *ABD*, vol. 2, 862.

[161] Michael L. Russo. Photographed by Michael James Russo, April 23, 2012.

[162] Salomon and Milner, *Jesus 2000*, 193.

The Via Dolorosa

derers, political or religious agitators, and others who had no rights.[163] Hellenistic history does not record the practice of crucifixion until the conquests of Alexander. He adopted the method of torture and death from the Persians. The Macedonian generals and administrators who succeeded Alexander the Great (diadochi) continued the practice of crucifixion.[164] It was also practiced under the Selucids by Antiochus Epiphanes and in Egypt under the Ptolmies. It is possible that the Greek town of Syracuse borrowed the practice from the Carthaginian, Denis the Tyrant. The Carthaginians frequently crucified people, and it is believed that the Romans adopted the practice of crucifixion from Carthage.[165]

Crucifixion was widespread in the ancient world and used as a political and military punishment. The main reason for its frequent use as a punishment by the Romans was its success as a deterrent. It was carried out publicly for all to

---

[163] Zugibe, "The Crucifixion of Jesus," 51; O'Collins, "Crucifixion," *ABD*, vol. 1, 1208; John R. Donahue, "Crucifixion," *EDB*, 298–299.

[164] Diadochi were the Macedonian generals and administrators who succeeded Alexander the Great. After Alexander's death in 323 BCE, they sought to increase their personal power. This created bloody power struggles. The Diadichi period ended with the defeat of Lysimachus at the hands of Seleucus I in 281 BCE. *The Columbia Encyclopedia*, 6th ed., s.v. "Diadochi" (New York, NY: Columbia University Press, 2001-2007). http://www.bartleby.com/65/di/Diadochi.html.

[165] Barbet, *A Doctor at Calvary*, 41–42. Barbet is crediting Father Holzmeister, SJ, with this information by referencing Father Holzmeister's study *Verbum Domini*, the review of the Pontifical Institute (May, July, August, September, 1934), under the title *Crux Domini Ejusque Crucifix ex Archaeological Romana Illustrantur*. R. Martin comments that the origins of crucifixion were not Roman, but the Roman's perfected it and brought it to a higher level than others throughout the Mediterranean. Martin, *Suffering of Love*, 86–87; Hengel, *Crucifixion*, 4–5; Donahue, "Crucifixion," *EDB*, 298; O'Collins, "Crucifixion," *ABD*, vol. 1, 1207.

The First Station: Jesus Is Condemned To Death

see that the crucified person (criminal) was receiving just punishment for the crime he or she was found guilty of committing. The Romans were confident that the fear created by crucifixion would keep the populace under control and prevent them from undermining the authority of the state. Crucifixion also satisfied the sadistic cruelty and overpowering desire for revenge of the individual rulers and officials in authority. M. Hengel points out, "Crucifixion is a manifestation of trans-subjective evil, a form of execution which manifests the demonic character of human cruelty and bestiality."[166] The Romans reserved crucifixion primarily for dangerous criminals and the lowest of slaves, but it was an effective deterrent for all. Most people would have been familiar with crucifixion since the Roman General Crassus crushed a rebellion in 71 BCE led by Sparticus and crucified six thousand slaves. Two thousand people were crucified in 4 BCE by the Roman General Varus when he put down a rebellion in Galilee.[167]

The Evangelists do not elaborate on any aspect of the crucifixion. They use words such as "scourging" and "crucifixion" but provide no further descriptions of what those words meant. Perhaps this is because those words were understood by all and no further embellishment was necessary. They frequently witnessed scourging and crucifixions. They, and the people they were writing to, knew the meaning by being eyewitnesses. Their firsthand experience

---

[166] Hengel, *Crucifixion*, 86–88; Martin, *Suffering of Love*, 87. In Paul's Letter to the Philippians, he reminds us that "He emptied Himself and took the form of a slave," Phil. 2:7. R. Holloway states that crucifixion was a means of intimidating the public and designed partly to entertain. Holloway, *A Death in Jerusalem*, 47.

[167] Walker, *In the Steps of Jesus*, 176–177; Donahue, "Crucifixion," *EDB*, 298; O'Collins, "Crucifixion," *ABD*, vol. 1, 1207–1208. O'Collins comments, "In Roman times, cultured writers preferred to say little about it (crucifixion)."

was enough to capture the full meaning. For us, however, the words have become less dramatic over time. With the exception of images we see through artists' renditions of Christ's Passion and death, we can paint no other definitive picture. The Scriptures are too sanitized for us to envision the horrors of Christ's Passion and death. We hear and read that Jesus suffered, Jesus died, and Jesus was scourged and accept the fact as somewhat routine. It is only through a thorough examination of the Roman practice of crucifixion that we can come to appreciate the true meaning of Christ's sacrifice.[168]

G. Rooney argues that the writers of Sacred Scripture were keenly focused on the details of Christ's sufferings. He illustrates that the Synoptic Gospels devote almost one-sixth of their text to the death of Jesus and the events that preceded it. John devoted almost one-third of his Gospel to Christ's Passion and death. The importance, according to Rooney, was to illustrate that Jesus is "The Way." Calvary was history's turning point. Jesus reversed human history, atoning for the sins of mankind and releasing a limitless outpouring of love. What happened on the cross at Calvary was the redemption of mankind. With Calvary, despair was replaced by hope.[169]

Actual proof of crucifixion was discovered in 1968 when Vassilios Tzaferis, a member of the Israel Antiquities Authority, excavated several tombs in the northern Jerusalem suburb of Giv'at Ha'Mivtar. In a first-century rock-hewn tomb, he found the remains of two men and a child. One of the men was sixty-five inches tall and in his mid-twenties. His right heel had been pierced by a four-and-a-half-inch nail. The head of the nail was still attached to a piece of olive wood. His legs had been spread and nailed to the side of the

---

[168] Barbet, *A Doctor at Calvary*, 8.

[169] Rooney, *The Mystery of Calvary*, 34, 35, 37.

The First Station: Jesus Is Condemned To Death

upright beam (known as the *stipes*). The board was nailed to the outside of the heel to prevent him from tearing his leg off the nail's small head. The nail was bent because it probably was hammered into the knotty part of the wood.

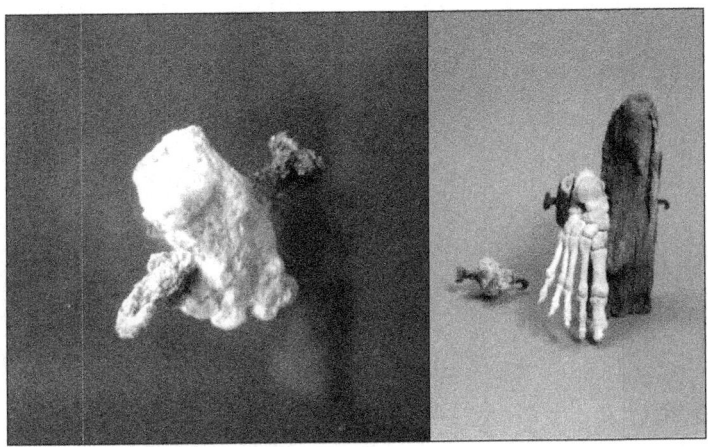

Figure 12. **Left:** Grim testimony to the manner of Jesus's death came to light in a Jewish cemetery in the northern Jerusalem suburb of Giv'at Ha-Mivtar. This foot bone is from a man identified as Yehochanan who died within decades of Jesus. It still holds the nail that pierced his foot when he was pinned to the cross.[170] **Right:** A demonstration of how Yehochanan's foot was pinned to the cross is shown next to the actual artifact.[171]

One speculates the family chose not to remove the nail for fear of tearing the foot. Unlike Jesus, the victim's arms were tied to cross. He most likely died slowly of asphyxiation, which was common in crucifixion. The man's name was scratched into the side of the ossuary. His name is Yehochanan (also Jehohanan), and he bears the title "The

---

[170] BAS, *Biblical World in Pictures*, photo NT88.

[171] Left; Todd Bolen/BiblePlaces.com, Anklebone of crucified man with nail, probably replica, tbs84289608. Right: Joe Zias, "Crucifixion in Antiquity, The Anthropological Evidence."

Crucified man of Giv'at Ha-Mivtar."[172] The Hebrew inscription on the ossuary reads "Jehohanan the son of HGQWL."[173]

Figure 13. The inscription found on the ossuary that identifies "Jehohanan the son of HGQWL."[174]

Returning to the account of Jesus's crucifixion, Pilate finally gave in to the demands of the Jews and handed Jesus over to be crucified. Although the case against Jesus was founded on lies (Luke 23:2), the Jewish leaders would not

---

[172] John Dominic Crossan, *Excavating Jesus, Beneath the Stones, Behind the Texts*, 246. Other references to this archaeological discovery can be found in Barry J. Beitzel and others, "Geography and History of the Bible Lands," in *BTBA*, 76; Peter Walker, *In the Steps of Jesus*, 177; M. C. Tenney and J. I. Packer, *Illustrated Manners and Customs*, 520.

[173] Zias, "Crucifixion in Antiquity." Zias uses the initials HGQWL but does not explain the meaning. According to J. Fitzmeyer, there is no satisfactory explanation of HGQWL. See Joseph A. Fitzmeyer, *To Advance the Gospel: New Testament Studies* (Grand Rapids, MI: Eerdmans Publishing Company, 1998), 126.

[174] Chandler Collins, Yehochanan Ossuary Inscription.

The First Station: Jesus Is Condemned To Death

accept a decision to acquit Him. Using Herod's decision as support, Pilate could not convince the crowd to set Jesus free.[175] Jesus, an innocent and prophetic man, was sentenced to death by one of the "cruelest forms of capital punishment that people had contrived to torment and degrade their enemies."[176] Before washing his hands and turning Jesus over to His executioners, Pilate performed one last duty that would antagonize the Jews. He ordered the inscription on the *titulus* to state, "Jesus of Nazareth, King of the Jews."[177] To ensure that the message would be read by all, the inscription was written in Aramaic, Latin, and Greek. Pilate was most likely annoyed that he felt forced to give in to the demands of the Jews and used the *titulus* as a means of passing along one last insult.[178] Nazareth was a very small town with a population of under three hundred people. It was so insignificant that it did not even warrant a place on the map. Nazareth was considered a "nothing" town. Pilate's insulting inscription could have been interpreted as stating, "This is Jesus of Nazareth (from nowhere), King of the Jews (who are nothing)."[179]

In spite of the objections screamed at him from the Jews, Pilate stated, "*Quod scripsi, scripsi*." That is, "What I have written, I have written (John 19:19–22)." Pilate, a representative of the greatest power on earth, ironically reaffirmed the kingship of Jesus and verified for all to see that Jesus

---

[175] Terrence Prendergast, "The Trial of Jesus, the Verdict of Pilate," *ABD*, vol. 5, 662.

[176] Pixner, *With Jesus in Jerusalem*, 135.

[177] Ibid., 136. A *titulus* was a sign (charge plate) that was affixed to the cross of the condemned. The crime of the accused was written on the *titulus*.

[178] Pixner, *With Jesus in Jerusalem*, 135–6.

[179] Richard Rohrbaugh, *Core Values of the Biblical World*, VHS, (*BAS*, 2000).

The Via Dolorosa

was a king.[180] Jesus is presented as the King of the Jews, but in reality it is the condemnation of the world that is taking place. In the action of the Jews who reject Jesus, it is the world condemning itself.[181] The Jews turned to Pilate for assistance in condemning Jesus. Pilate turned to Herod who, in turn, sent Jesus back to Pilate. Again, Pilate attempted to release Jesus. Pilate's hand washing sent the message that he did not want anything to do with the verdict.

> So Judas who, through "repentance," brings back the money (though indeed it is not accepted); so the Jews who do not put the blood-money in the Temple treasury but use it to acquire a burial-ground for strangers (!) [sic]; so in the game of exchanges, Pilate who more than any of the others, would have liked to release the prisoner; so Herod who, disappointed in the entertainment he had hoped for, sent back the condemned man; so the leaders of the people who invoke their lack of political authorization to judge the issue (John 8:31) whilst Pilate, constrained to pronounce judgment by political pressure of the gravest kind (John 19:12) declines to accept any moral responsibility (Matthew 27:24). No one wishes to be responsible. That is why they are all guilty.[182]

They were all unaware that the Light of the World was in their midst. They were about to kill the Son of God. In doing so, they unknowingly set into motion the events that saved mankind. The very reason Jesus came into this world was about to be played out in all its horror: to suffer and die for the sins of all mankind. Their actions formed in anger and hatred would open the floodgates of love and let hope shine once again in the world.

---

[180] Brown, *A Crucified Christ*, 64.
[181] De La Potterie, SJ, *The Hour of Jesus*, 85–6.
[182] Von Balthasar, *Mysterium Paschale*, 115.

CHAPTER 8

THE SECOND STATION: JESUS CARRIES HIS CROSS

So they took Jesus, and carrying the cross Himself He went out to what is called the Place of the Skull, in Hebrew, Golgotha. (John 19:17)

𝒮acred Scripture presents a heartbreaking picture of the kingship of Christ. He is not leading armies or receiving the homage of princes and dignitaries. He is torn and bleeding. He is so helpless that He cannot even brush the flies from His wounds.[183] The picture of Jesus that John presents to us, however, differs from that of the Synoptic Gospels. In John's Gospel, Jesus is not a broken man, a fugitive, or a condemned victim. In John's Gospel, Jesus is presented as one who dominates the events. Jesus proceeds with authority and majesty. He is the master of the situation. He is the one who takes the initiative. In the scene in the Garden of Gethsemane, we see that it is not the Roman soldiers who give the commands: it is Jesus. Of His own free will, Jesus goes to meet His adversaries. "It is Jesus who determines

---

[183] Holloway, *A Death in Jerusalem*, 22.

when His hour must come."[184] Jesus, the Lamb of God, steps up and takes His Cross.

Experts agree that there were various types of crosses used for crucifixion. The Romans used at least two different yet similar types. One style was in the form of a T. This was called the *crux commissa*. The second cross of choice was called the *crux immissa* and was in the shape of a *cruciform* †. Whichever style was chosen, the custom was for the victim to carry the cross beam, which was called the *patibulum*.[185] Generally, the cross was made in two pieces. The trunk of the cross was called the *stipes*. This can also be referred to as a *stake* or a *pale*. In ancient times, the Latin word for cross, *crux*, or the Greek word σταυρός meant a *stake* or *pale* that was fixed vertically into the ground. This became a permanent fixture called the *stipes crucis*. The word *crux* eventually came to mean the combination of two pieces of wood. There were times when just a *stake* or *pale* was used. Josephus tells us that Titus just used *stakes* when he crucified five hundred Jews daily. In those instances, the hands were nailed above the head.[186]

There is much debate as to whether Jesus carried the complete cross (*stipes* and *patibulum* assembled) or just the *patibulum*. According to the Roman custom, Jesus would only have carried the *patibulum*. He would not have carried the full cross as we see in artistic renditions of the crucifixion.[187] The victim, his shoulders and back beaten raw and his

---

[184] De La Potterie, SJ, *The Hour of Jesus*, 29, 33.

[185] Holloway, *A Death in Jerusalem*, 35. Additional descriptions for various types of crosses can be found in Zugibe, *The Crucifixion of Jesus*, 40–41; O'Collins, "Crucifixion," *ABD*, 1208; Donahue, "Crucifixion," in *EDB*, 298.

[186] Holloway, *A Death in Jerusalem*, 40; O'Collins, "Crucifixion," *ABD*, vol. 1, 1208.

[187] Barbet, *A Doctor at Calvary*, 55; Zugibe, *The Crucifixion of Jesus*, 40–41; *Crucifixion*, DVD, A&E Networks; *The Crucifixion of*

The Second Station: Jesus Carries His Cross

skin shredded to the bone, was tied to a rough beam of wood and forced to carry it to the place of execution.[188] The cross that is featured by most artists would have been very complex and required specific carpentry skills. That cross would have weighed approximately two hundred pounds. This would have made it close to impossible for a person who had been scourged as Jesus was to carry it. P. Barbet suggests that Jesus did not drag the cross to Calvary; He carried it. Barbet states "One finds in all the texts *"portare* (Latin, meaning "to carry"), *bajulare* (Latin, meaning "to carry" or "bear a burden"), and *bastazein,* (Greek, meaning "carry") to carry, but never, *"trahare* (Latin, meaning "to draw"), or *surein,* (Greek, meaning to drag, pull, or draw)."[189] In view of the number of crucifixions that were being performed at any given time (hundreds or even thousands), it is unlikely that the more complex cross was used.[190]

Christ, A Return to the Cross, 2004, DVD, Bema Publishing; *How Jesus Died, the Final 18 Hours,* DVD, Trinity Pictures, Ltd., 2004); O'Collins, "Crucifixion," *ABD,* vol.1, 1208-1209.

[188] Holloway, *A Death in Jerusalem,* 36.

[189] Barbet, *A Doctor at Calvary,* 49.

[190] Zugibe, *The Crucifixion of Jesus,* 40–41.

The Via Dolorosa

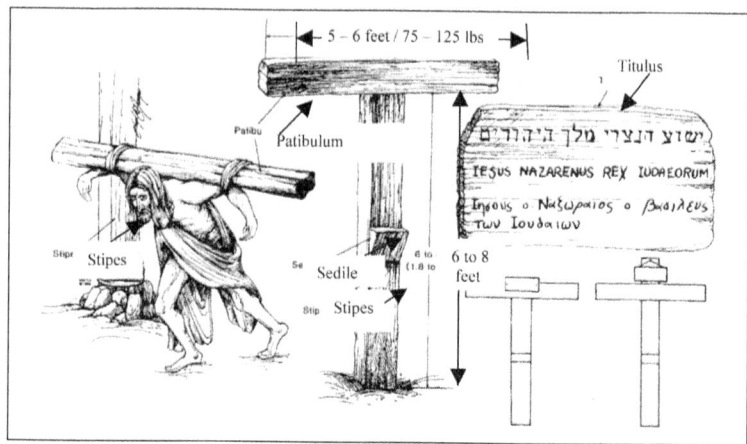

Figure 14. **Left:** The victim carries the *patibulum* to the site of the *stipes*. **Center:** An example of the T cross (the *crux commissa*). This was the cross that was commonly used by the Romans. **Upper Right:** An example of the *titulus* stating the name of Jesus and His crime. **Lower Right:** Possible methods for attaching the *titulus* to the cross. The cross on the left is the T cross and the cross on the right is the *cruciform* † or "Latin cross."[191]

Figure 15. An example of first-century CE crosses. The *patibulum* would be positioned onto the *stipes*, which was already placed in the ground. The *titulus* would be attached above the head of the victim.[192]

---

[191] Edwards, and others, "The Physical Death of Jesus Christ."

[192] Todd Bolen/BiblePlaces.com, Three crosses at Tantur, tbs80019402. The Jehovah Witness official web site states the Christ

The Second Station: Jesus Carries His Cross

There has also been considerable debate concerning how the cross was carried. Did Jesus carry the full-size cross that included the *stipes* and *patibulum* or did he just carry the *patibulum*? If He only carried the *patibulum*, were His arms affixed to it with ropes or did He carry it over His shoulder? J. Donahue argues that Jesus was expected to carry the transverse beam of the cross. G. O'Collins states that the victims would have carried a cross or at least a transverse beam.[193] The Gospels are not specific on this point, but we do get some idea. All four Evangelists tell us that Jesus carried His own cross when He left the Praetorium. It soon became evident that Jesus was too weak to continue carrying the heavy cross, and Simon the Cyrenean was pressed into service.

Given the information that we have about crucifixion under the Romans, the scenario indicates that Jesus was carrying the *patibulum* on His shoulder and was not tied to it. A victim would be tied to the *patibulum* to prevent him from creating any violent reaction or incident. The soldiers

---

was crucified on a single stake. See "Did Jesus Really Die on a Cross?" http://www.watchtower.org/e/200604a/article_01.htm. Donahue, in "Crucifixion," *EDB*, 298, 299, makes reference to the use of a stake or tree for crucifixion. However, he references Scripture (Mark 15:21; Luke 24:39; John 20:27) to state that Christ was crucified on a cross. Martin Hengel does not discuss the use of a stake. He states that the victim was nailed to the cross "with outstretched arms." Hengel, *Crucifixion*, 25. O'Collins also references the use of a stake, "At times the cross was only one vertical stake." He adds, "Josephus lets us see that there was no fixed pattern for crucifying people. Much depended on the sadistic ingenuity of the moment." O'Collins, "Crucifixion" *ABD*, 1208–9. I can find no credible support for the Jehovah Witness position that Jesus was nailed to a single stake.

[193] Donahue, "Crucifixion," *EDB*, 299; O'Collins, "Crucifixion," *ABD*, 1208–1209; Daniel J. Harrington, SJ, states "Simon was forced to carry the crossbeam." Harrington, "The Gospel of Mark," *NJBC* §41-105 *Crucifixion*, 628.

may have realized that Jesus was in such a downtrodden and weakened state after the scourging that He was physically incapable of becoming violent and uncontrollable. Therefore, they chose to not secure His arms to the *patibulum*. Also, there was no reason to bind a free man such as Simon to the *patibulum*. Because Luke adds that Simon was carrying the cross behind Jesus, this suggests that Jesus was walking in front, escorted by the soldiers, and that Simon was behind Him carrying the *patibulum*.[194]

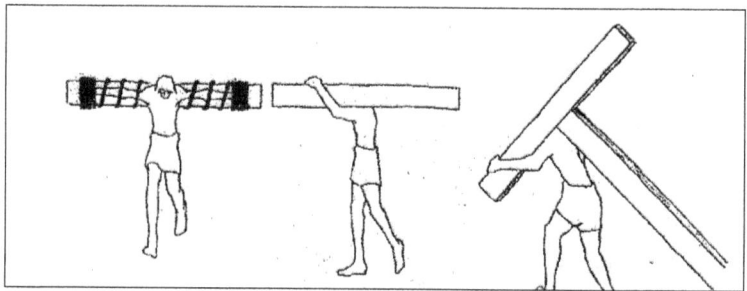

Figure 16. **Left:** The victim carrying the *patibulum* with his arms tied. **Center:** The victim carrying the *patibulum* over his shoulder. **Right:** The entire cross is carried by the victim. This was very rare.[195]

Most experts agree that that the *patibulum* was carried by the victim to the place of crucifixion. The *patibulum* weighed approximately fifty to sixty pounds. Reports indicate that the Romans had as many as one thousand *stipes* in place at a given time. It is unlikely that the victims would be

---

[194] Barbet, *A Doctor at Calvary*, 55–56.

[195] Zugibe, *The Crucifixion of Jesus*, 48; Donahue, "Crucifixion," *EDB*, 299; O'Collins, "Crucifixion," *ABD*, vol. 1, 1208–1209. For those who believe the Shroud of Turin is the burial shroud of Christ, Zugibe comments that there is an abrasion on the right shoulder of the shroud. In addition, the right shoulder appears to be lower than the left shoulder. In his opinion, the abrasions are consistent with carrying the *patibulum* on the right shoulder. Zugibe, *The Crucifixion of Jesus*, 195.

The Second Station: Jesus Carries His Cross

able to carry the full weight of the cross as depicted by art and in Hollywood presentations.[196]

We see the dignity and majesty in Jesus as He takes His cross. It is the same dignity and majesty He demonstrated during His questioning by Annas. It is the same dignity and majesty He demonstrated when He received the blow on the face. The entire trial before Pilate is an example of the dignity and majesty of Jesus. The Way of the Cross becomes a triumphal march. The cross becomes a throne, and Jesus accepts his cross lovingly and with great dignity from His Father's hand. He is fully aware of His mission and does not go to the cross passively or with a struggle.[197] Jesus goes to the cross as a sacrificial lamb, not as a fearful man of power. R. Holloway explains, "In Jesus there is a meaning and disclosure about God; what we could not find out about ourselves, God disclosed for us in Jesus. He is the truth about God, and we see that truth at its most harrowing and unacceptable in the cross. The cross is also the truth about God. It shows the manner of the exercise of the power of God. It shows that God rules by love and not by power."[198] This statement could be summed up by the old adage "love conquers all." What could be more powerful than a love that conquers death and redeems us from our sins?

---

[196] Zugibe, *The Crucifixion of Jesus*, 46; O'Collins, "Crucifixion," *ABD*, 1209; Hengel and Donahue also discuss the hundreds and thousands of crucifixions that were carried out daily. This number would require that many *stipes* be in place to crucify so many persons.

[197] De La Potterie, *The Hour of Jesus*, 19.

[198] Holloway, *A Death in Jerusalem*, 23.

CHAPTER 9

THE THIRD STATION: JESUS FALLS FOR THE FIRST TIME

Behold the Lamb of God, who takes away the sin of the world. (John 1:29)

This third Station is among the traditional Stations of the Cross recognized by Christian pilgrims. It is not referenced in Sacred Scripture and was not included by Pope John Paul II when he prayed the Stations of the Cross at the Roman Colosseum on Good Friday in 1991. The word "falls" resonates for Christians and conjures up a variety of images. For some, it is a reminder of our own failings and difficulties, and for others, it is a reference to man's first disobedience before God—man's sin in the Garden of Eden.[199]

To fully understand the physical condition of Jesus at the moment of His first fall, one must recall the events in the Garden of Gethsemane. Most Christians do not recognize the full impact of what transpired in that Garden. Jesus

---

[199] Holloway, *A Death in Jerusalem*, 37.

The Third Station: Jesus Falls For The First Time

did not only endure severe mental anguish that drained His physical strength to the point of total exhaustion. The *hematidrosis* that Jesus experienced and the anxiety associated with it were contributing factors to His weakened condition. The effects of the *hematidrosis* were a general weakness, depression, dehydration, and low blood and fluid volume (*hypovolemia*) caused by His sweating and blood loss.

Following the scourging, Jesus's condition was grave. He was in the early stages of traumatic or injury shock due to the severe beating. The beating to the chest wall would have impacted His lungs and caused fluid buildup. He would have been experiencing difficulty breathing and been in severe pain. Beating with a *flagrum* would have caused rib fractures, serious lung bruises, and lacerations that would have bled into the chest cavity. It was common for the victim to suffer bouts of vomiting, tremors, and seizures combined with periods of fainting during the scourging. "The victim would be reduced to an exhausted, mangled mass of flesh and would be craving for water. The scourging propelled Jesus into an early stage of shock."[200]

The crown of thorns added to the extreme suffering Jesus was already experiencing. To fully understand the gravity of this, one must have some knowledge of the nerve supply to the head. "The nerve supply for pain reception to the head region is distributed by branches of two major nerves: the *trigeminal nerve*, which essentially supplies the front half of the head, and the *greater occipital branch*, which supplies the back half of the head."[201]

Matthew tells us that the soldiers mocked Jesus and struck him on the head with a reed (Matt. 27:30). Because

---

[200] Zugibe, *The Crucifixion of Jesus*, 15, 22, 23. For further medical information concerning the preliminary sufferings see Barbet, *A Doctor at Calvary*, 81–91. Hengel, O'Collins, and Donahue agree that the scourging would have caused profuse bleeding and extreme loss of blood.

[201] Zugibe, *The Crucifixion of Jesus*, 33.

the crown was in the shape of a hat covering Jesus's head, this would have put a large number of long thorns in contact with the entire top of His head. The result would have brought about pain similar to that of being branded by a hot poker or that of an electric shock. The medical term for this type of nerve irritation is *trigeminal neuralgia*. According to Doctor Robert Nugent, professor and chairman of the Department of Neurosurgery at West Virginia University School of Medicine and a pioneer in treating patients with *trigeminal neuralgia*, "Trigeminal neuralgia is said to be the worst pain that man is heir to. It is a devastating pain that is just unbearable in its several forms."[202]

For those who accept the authenticity of the Shroud of Turin as the burial shroud of Jesus, much information can be gained from the findings of the studies and the tests done upon it. Jesus may have received thirty-nine lashes of the *flagrum*. However, the *flagrum* consisted of three thongs. Each lash would have caused three marks on His body. The math is simple. Thirty-nine lashes multiplied by three thongs, totals one hundred and seventeen lash marks. If the *flagrum* consisted of more than three thongs, there would have been more lash marks. It was against Mosaic Law to exceed forty lashes (Deut. 25:3). However, the Romans had no laws governing this punishment. The lash marks on the Shroud of Turin exceed one hundred and are found on the front and back of the trunk as well as the legs down to the calves.[203]

For Jesus, the journey to Calvary must have seemed like it would never end. As He walked He experienced waves of excruciating pain. His lungs must have felt as though they

---

[202] Ibid., 33–34. O'Collins and Donahue both discuss the excruciating pain experienced by the crucified victim. See Donahue, "Crucifixion," *EDB*, 298–299; O'Collins, "Crucifixion," *ABD*, vol. 1, 1207–1210.

[203] Zugibe, *The Crucifixion of Jesus*, 22; Gaertner, "Scourging," *EDB*, 1173.

The Third Station: Jesus Falls For The First Time

were bursting. His head was in raging pain, and He may have been slipping in and out of consciousness along the route. This scene presents a truly sorrowful picture for those meditating on Jesus's Passion and death. However, there is a much more powerful view of this tragedy. "What we see as a falling in the dust is in fact a rising up and a standing against every power that ranges against God. Christ falls, but only to lift us up."[204]

Today, the third Station of the Cross is marked by two broken columns. With the help of donations from Polish soldiers who were visiting the Holy Land in 1947, a chapel was built on the spot to commemorate where Jesus, according to tradition, fell for the first time.

Figure 17. **Left:** The two broken columns that mark the spot where tradition says that Jesus fell for the first time. **Right:** A view of the interior of the Polish Roman Catholic Chapel built on the site of the second Station of the Cross.[205]

---

[204] Holloway, *A Death in Jerusalem*, 46.

[205] Michael L. Russo. Photographed by Michael James Russo. Photo on the left, April 23, 2012. Photo on the right, April 25, 2012.

CHAPTER 10

THE FOURTH STATION: JESUS MEETS HIS MOTHER

> *Behold this child is destined for the fall and rise of many in Israel, and to be a sign that will be contradicted (and you yourself a sword will pierce) so that the thoughts of many hearts may be revealed. (Luke 2:35)*

There is no scriptural reference for Mary meeting her Son at the fourth Station of the Cross. However, this is not to suggest that Mary and the role she plays in salvation history is nowhere to be found in Sacred Scripture. There is no other person who has ever had such a close relationship with Jesus throughout His life. "Mary is a believer who has been with Jesus from His conception, to His birth, His infancy, childhood, and manhood."[206] It is difficult, if not impossible, to think of Mary without thinking of Jesus. It is from Mary that Jesus received His humanity. Perhaps His eyes were the same color or His nose the same shape. He may even have shared the same smile and expressions. Mary

---

[206] Bertrand Buby, SM, *Mary of Galilee*, vol. 1 (Staten Island, NY: Alba House, 1994), 106.

The Fourth Station: Jesus Meets His Mother

taught Jesus to speak, guided His first steps, and kissed His cuts and bruises just as any mother would do for her child. Mary and Jesus shared the unique bond that exists between mother and son, yet there were still some events that she "pondered in her heart," as Luke 2:19 tells us.[207] We cannot forget that "the Word became flesh," as John's Gospel states in his prologue (John 1:14). The Word became flesh in a very specific way in the womb of Mary.[208]

It does not have to be written in Scripture that Mary suffered along with Jesus and followed along the painful path to Calvary with her Son. From the previous discussion, one can safely assume and believe that Mary felt the "full thrust of the sword" pierce her heart as she followed her Son. Scripture does tell us that Jesus's friends abandoned Him. It is only Mary, the mother of Jesus; her sister, Mary Clopas; and Mary Magdalene along with John who remained at the foot of the cross. At an earlier time, His mother stood next to Him at the manger, and her soul was filled with heavenly music. Now, she was hearing the crowds shout insults and vulgarities at her beloved Son.[209]

We cannot, therefore, underestimate the role that Mary played in the life of Jesus. Jesus has His mother to thank for His human self-consciousness. Hans Urs von Balthasar reminds us it was Jesus's mother who introduced her Son to the meaning and the depths of Israel's religion. Mary introduced her Son to the covenant that trained Him for His messianic office. His own knowledge of the Father's mission in the Holy Spirit showed Him what He had to do, and at that point, the relationship with His mother became reversed.

---

[207] Richard John Neuhaus, *Death on a Friday Afternoon* (New York, NY: Basic Books, 2000), 75.

[208] Ibid., 84.

[209] Thomas Á Kempis, *On the Passion of Christ According to the Four Evangelists* (San Francisco, CA: Ignatius Press, 2004), 114.

The Via Dolorosa

Now Jesus educated His mother about the greatness of his task. He cultivated the maturity she needed to be able to stand with Him at the cross.[210]

The fourth Station of the Cross is located in a chapel that is marked by a lintel depicting Jesus meeting His mother. Close to this lintel is the Armenian Catholic Church that was built in 1881. The Church was dedicated to Mary and is named the Armenian Church of Our Lady of the Spasm. There is a mosaic floor inside the church that was discovered during its building. The floor may belong to a church that was constructed in the fifth or sixth century. The center of the mosaic is said to contain the outline of Mary's sandals, marking the spot where she stood as Jesus passed by.[211]

Figure 18. **Left:** The lintel showing Jesus meeting His mother. **Right:** Interior view of the Armenian Church of Our Lady of the Spasm. Note the arrow designating the sandal imprints.[212]

---

[210] Hans Urs von Balthasar, Joseph Cardinal Ratzinger, *Mary the Church at the Source* (San Francisco, CA: Ignatius Press, 2005), 103, 107.

[211] Salomon, Milner, *Jesus 2000*, 194; Jacobs, *Israel and the Palestine Territories*, 331; Rivka Gonen, *Biblical Holy Places: An Illustrated Guide* (Mahwah, NJ: Paulist Press, 2000), 173.

[212] Michael L. Russo. Photographed by Michael James Russo. Left photo April 23, 2012. Right photo April 25, 2012.

The Fourth Station: Jesus Meets His Mother

The sandals were mentioned in a fourteenth-century text as marking the spot. However, there is no proof that this is credible evidence and should be considered alongside traditional legends. That is, they are traditional legends that have no biblical or archaeological support for their authenticity.

CHAPTER 11

THE FIFTH STATION: SIMON THE CYRENE HELPS JESUS

They pressed into service a passer-by, Simon, a Cyrenean, who was coming in from the country, the father of Alexander and Rufus, to carry His cross. (Mark 15:21)

Simon was a Jew born in Cyrene (North Africa). Although it is not clear as to why he was in Jerusalem, one can assume that he was visiting the city for the Passover feast. However, it is uncertain as to whether he was a pilgrim or a permanent resident.[213] Cyrene was the capital of the North African Roman province of Cyrenaica. Cyrenaica had been settled by the Greeks in the seventh century BCE and came under Roman rule in 96 BCE. During the first half of the first century BCE, Cyrene (modern-day Libya) and Crete were joined together to form Cyrenaica, a new Roman senatorial province. There was a significant Jewish

---

[213] Daniel J. Harrington, "The Gospel According to Mark," in *NJBC*, §41:105, 628.

community in Cyrene dating back to the early Hellenistic period.[214]

The Synoptic Gospels infer that Simon did not have a choice in helping Jesus to carry the cross. Both Matthew and Mark state that Simon was "pressed (ἠγγάρευσα meaning "forced" or "compelled") into service" (Matt. 27:32; Mark 15:21). Luke tells us "As they led Him away they took hold of a certain Simon, a Cyrenian, who was coming in from the country; and after laying the cross on him, they made him carry it behind Jesus" (Luke 23:26). John has Jesus carrying the cross by Himself and does not mention Simon (John 19:17). Considering the physical state that Jesus was in at this stage of the journey to Calvary, the Roman soldiers realized that, if Jesus was to make it to Calvary alive, He was going to need some assistance. Selecting someone to carry the cross for Jesus suggests that His arms were not tied to the *patibulum* and that the He was carrying the beam on His shoulders. There would have been no legal reason for the Roman soldiers to bind a free man such as Simon.

It would have been futile for Simon to refuse the order to carry the cross. Because Simon's sons Alexander and Rufus are both mentioned in Scripture (Mark 15:21), it appears that Simon eventually became a member of the Christian community. In 1942, an ossuary was found in an ancient grave in the Kidron Valley. The name engraved on the ossuary was "Alexander, Son of Simon the Cyrenean [sic]."[215]

---

[214] Richard E. Oster, Jr., "Cyrene," *EDB*, 305; W. Ward Gasque, "Cyrene," *ABD*, vol. 1, 1230.

[215] Pixner, *With Jesus in Jerusalem*, 139; W. Edward Glenny, "Simon," *EDB*, 1224.

The Via Dolorosa

Figure 19. **Left:** The area where it is believed Simon of Cyrene was pressed into service to help Jesus carry His cross. **Right:** The entrance to the chapel where Simon helped Jesus. The circular area of paving stones marks the location where Simon took the cross from Jesus. The chapel was built by the Franciscans in 1885.[216]

---

[216] Michael L. Russo. Photographed by Michael James Russo, April 23, 2012.

CHAPTER 12

THE SIXTH STATION: VERONICA WIPES THE FACE OF JESUS

Everyone who acknowledges me before others I will acknowledge before my heavenly Father. (Matt. 10:32)

The story of a woman named Veronica wiping the face of Jesus is not found in the Gospels. According to tradition, as Jesus carried His cross along the path to Calvary, a woman in the crowd is said to have stepped forward to offer Jesus a cloth so that He could wipe the blood and sweat from His face. Once she wiped the face of Christ, His image was left on her cloth. The woman's name was Veronica. In Latin, the words *vera icon* mean "true image."

Another legend claims that the Emperor Tiberius was very ill and invited Veronica to Rome. After he viewed the cloth bearing the image of Christ's face, Tiberius was healed. There is another story that places Veronica at Jesus's trial before Pilate. A woman named Veronica testified on behalf of Jesus. She said, "I was afflicted with an issue of blood twelve years, and I touched the hem of His garments, and presently the issue of my blood stopped."[217] This is supposed to be the same woman with the issue of blood found in the accounts of all three Synoptic writers (cf. Matt. 9:20–22; cf. Mark 5:25–29; cf. Luke 8:43–44)). There is no proof that any of these stories or legends are factual. However, faithful pilgrims have kept them alive over the centuries.

If there is such veil the exact location of it is unknown. There are stories claiming that Veronica's veil is kept at the Vatican in Rome. However, on September 1, 2006, Pope Benedict XVI visited Manoppello, Italy, where a group of Capuchin monks claim to have the veil. The Pope did not proffer an opinion as to the authenticity of the veil and did not remark that one was at the Vatican. He commented that his visit was so that "we can try to better know the face of our Lord, so that from it we can find strength in love and peace that can show us the path."[218]

The sixth Station of the Cross is marked by a column that is recessed in a wall. The section was purchased by the

---

[217] Anonymous, *The Gospel of Nicodemus Formerly Called the Acts of Pontius Pilate*, (Whitefish, MT: Kessinger Publishing, 2004), Chapter V, #26, 12; reference to Veronica's veil healing the Emperor Tiberius and being kept at the Vatican is mentioned in Salomon and Milner, *Jesus 2000*, 194. See Antoine Dégert, "Saint Veronica," in *The Catholic Encyclopedia*, vol. 15. http://www.newadvent.org/cathen/15362.htm. For additional reference to Veronica as the woman with the issue of blood and the alleged healing of the Emperor Tiberius, see John Oliver Hand and Petrus Christus, "Salve sancta facies: Some Thoughts on the Iconography of the *Head of Christ*," *Metropolitan Museum Journal*, vol. 27 (1992), 10; James F. Rhodes, "The Pardoner's Vernycle and His Vera Icon," *Modern Language Studies*, vol. 13, no.2 (1963), 34–40. See "The Euangelium Nichodemi and Vindicta Saluatoris in Anglo-Saxon England," in *Two Old English Apocrypha and Their Manuscript Source*, ed. J. E. Cross (Cambridge: Cambridge University Press, 1996), 72–74 for additional reference to the Veronica legend..

[218] "Pope in Visit to Religious Relic.," *BBC News*, 1 September 2006. http://news.bbc.co.uk/2/hi/europe/5305592.stm.

The Sixth Station: Veronica Wipes The Face Of Jesus

Greek Catholics in 1883, and the Church of St. Veronica was built in 1885. It is believed that the Church of St. Veronica was built over the remains of a sixth-century church.[219] This church is also called the Church of the Holy Face. It is part of the Crusader monastery of St. Cosmos. Antonio Barluzzi refurbished the church in 1953 and paid special attention to restoring the Crusader arches in the chapel. The church is maintained by the Little Sisters, a Greek Catholic rite.

Figure 20. **Left:** The column marking the spot where Veronica wiped the face of Jesus. **Right:** The interior of the Church of the Holy Face. Note the refurbished Crusader arches.[220]

---

[219] Salomon and Milner, *Jesus 2000*, 194.

[220] Michael L. Russo. Photographed by Michael James Russo, Left photo April 23, 2012. Right photo April 25, 2012.

CHAPTER 13

THE SEVENTH STATION: JESUS FALLS FOR THE SECOND TIME

There is no salvation through anyone else, nor is there any other name under heaven given to the human race by which we are to be saved. (Acts 4:12)

According to forensic pathologist Dr. Frederick Zugibe, at this time along the journey to Calvary, Jesus would have been almost numb with exhaustion. The physical effects of the journey would be taking their toll. The mental anguish and physical sufferings He endured in the Garden of Gethsemane combined with the effects of the brutal flogging at the Praetorium and the nerve-racking pains from the crown of thorns had drained what strength He had. His exhaustion would be accompanied by a marked shortness of breath. He had not eaten since the previous night and lost a tremendous amount of body fluid. In His weakened condition, the noon sun would have added to the difficulty and induced intense weakness and dizziness. It would not be unusual for Him to stumble and fall several times. Although

The Seventh Station: Jesus Falls For The Second Time

the Stations of the Cross initiated by St. Francis of Assisi show Jesus falling only three times, there is little doubt that His condition caused Him to fall many times. His weakened condition must have been obvious to the Roman soldiers early on because they pressed Simon the Cyrenean into service at the fifth Station.[221] Isaiah gives us a good idea of the state Jesus was in: "From the sole of the foot to the head there is no sound spot: wound and welt and gaping gash, not drained, or bandaged, or eased with salve (Isaiah 1:6)."

The seventh Station of the Cross is known as the Judgment Gate. The station is located on the north-south street called *Khan ez-Zeit*, which is a major market in the Old City of Jerusalem. The chapel at this location belongs to the Coptic Church. Inside the chapel is a column that has survived from the double row of columns that outlined the length of the Cardo Maximus, which was the main street of the Roman city. Legend tells us that this is where Jesus fell for the second time.[222]

---

[221] Zugibe, *The Crucifixion of Jesus*, 48.

[222] Michael L. Russo. Photographed by Michael James Russo, April 23, 2012. The letter to the Hebrews also mentions the sufferings of Jesus outside the city gate. Heb. 13:12.

The Via Dolorosa

Figure 21. The Judgment Gate marks the spot where legend tells us Jesus fell for the second time. The double doors behind the semi-circle of paving stones lead to the chapel belonging to the Copts.[223]

Figure 22. Remnants of the Cardo Maximus today.[224]

---

[223] Salomon and Milner, *Jesus 2000*, 194. Photo: Studium Biblicum Franciscanum. http://198.62.75.1/www1/ofm/sbf/escurs/Ger/09escursEn.html.

[224] Todd Bolen/BiblePlaces.com, Cardo from southeast, tb051906305.

CHAPTER 14

THE EIGHTH STATION: JESUS MEETS THE WOMEN OF JERUSALEM

Daughters of Jerusalem, do not weep for me, but weep for yourselves and for your children. (Luke 23:28)

Women played a more active and nobler role in the Passion and death of Jesus than men. Jesus met His mother in the fourth Station. Veronica approached Him in the sixth Station. He spoke to the women of Jerusalem in the eighth Station, and His mother received His dead body in her arms at the thirteenth Station. With the exception of John, the disciples abandoned Christ, leaving the women to provide support. The fact that Jesus acknowledged women in public was extraordinary. The custom of the time was that a man should not address any woman in a public place, not even his wife. There was a real contempt for women at that time. However, it was modified in many cases by the love that existed between spouses and other family members. One

The Via Dolorosa

of the prayers prayed daily at the synagogue stated, "Blessed art thou, O Lord . . . who hast not made me a woman."[225]

Women had very few rights and could be divorced by their husbands for frivolous reasons. Christ's attitude toward women was one of openness and caring. Jesus brought freshness and a freedom to His teaching about God's relationship to men and women. This attitude shocked and disturbed many, and it most likely contributed to His fate.[226] Scripture tells us that humanity is made in the image of God. Humanity is male and female, and Jesus treated each equally.

The warning that Jesus gave to the women of Jerusalem represents a continuation of the theme of the destruction of the city of Jerusalem. Jesus predicted the destruction of Jerusalem as He entered the city.[227]

> As He drew near, He saw the city and wept over it, saying, "If this day you only knew what makes for peace—but now it is hidden from your eyes. For the days are coming upon you when your enemies will raise a palisade against you; they will encircle you and hem you in on all sides. They will smash you to the ground and your children within you, and they will not leave one stone upon another within you because you did not recognize the time of your visitation. (Luke 19:41–44).

When confronted with the women who were mourning and weeping, Jesus turned to them and said,

> Daughters of Jerusalem, do not weep for me; weep instead for yourselves and for your children, for indeed,

---

[225] Holloway, *A Death in Jerusalem*, 49–50.

[226] Ibid., 50.

[227] Raymond E. Brown, SS, *An Introduction to the New Testament* (New York, NY: Doubleday, 1997), 259.

The Eighth Station: Jesus Meets The Women Of Jerusalem

the days are coming when people will say, "Blessed are the barren, the wombs that never bore and the breasts that never nursed." At that time people will say to the mountains, "Fall upon us!" and to the hills, "Cover us!" for if these things are done when the wood is green what will be happen when it is dry? (Luke 23:28–32).

According to R. Brown, "The specification 'yourselves and your children' recognizes that the burden of the coming catastrophe will fall on another generation."[228] Jerusalem was completely destroyed in 70 CE.[229]

The eighth Station of the Cross is found outside of the Second Temple Period city limits. This tells us that Jesus's meeting with the women of Jerusalem must have taken place in the open field on the way to Calvary. The Station is marked by a stone bearing a cross and a Latin inscription. The inscription reads, "Jesus Christ Victorious." The marker is embedded in the wall of the Monastery of St. Cara-

---

[228] Brown, *An Introduction to the New Testament*, 259.
[229] See Chapter 5, page 27.

lambos.²³⁰ This particular location is near Golgotha, but its access is blocked by a Greek Orthodox Church.²³¹

Figure 23. Station VIII is marked by a stone bearing a cross. The inscription reads "Jesus Christ Victorious."²³²

---

²³⁰ St. Caralambos (Charalambos, or Haralambos), a Greek Orthodox priest, lived at the time of the Emperor Septimus Severus (194–211 CE) in the city of Magnesia near Ephesus. He won many souls for Christ through preaching and instruction. Others, including Governor Lucian, Porphyrius, and Baptus, converted when they witnessed astonishing miracles while torturing St. Caralambos. He suffered many tortures and withstood all of them. He was 107 years old when he was martyred on February 10, which is his feast day. Adapted from *The Synaxarion: The Lives of the Saints of the Orthodox Church*, vol. 3, compiled by Hieromonk Makarios of Simonos Petra and translated from the French by Christopher Hookway (Chalkidike, Greece: Holy Convent of the Annunciation of Our Lady, 2001) 463–466. http://www.goarch.org/en/special/listen-Learn_share/haralambos/learn/index.asp.

²³¹ Salomon and Milner, *Jesus 2000*, 194.

²³² Michael L. Russo. Photographed by Michael James Russo, April 23, 2012.

CHAPTER 15

THE NINTH STATION: JESUS FALLS FOR THE THIRD TIME

But Israel does not know, my people has not understood. Ah! Sinful nation, people laden with wickedness, evil race, corrupt children! They have forsaken the Lord, spurned the Holy One of Israel, apostatized. (Isaiah 1:3–4)

*J*esus's slow and painful journey to the cross continues. F. Zugibe's forensic analysis suggests that Jesus's breathing was becoming more labored; fluid was accumulating around and within His lungs. It is possible that He was suffering from pneumothorax (collapsing of the lung or lungs) from the vicious scourging as well as the effects of the journey to Calvary. Each time He staggered, tripped, or fell, His pain increased. He suffered extreme pain in all His muscles and joints. It was getting increasingly difficult to go on and extremely difficult to get up each time He fell. His clothing was most likely stuck to His body by the clotted blood from the open wounds of the scourging.[233]

Along the road in the direction of the Church of the Holy Sepulchre is a staircase ascending to the roof of the Church of the Holy Sepulchre. Another column that has survived from the Roman Cardo Maximus marks the place where Jesus fell for the third time. The column is between the gates of the Ethiopian monastery (Deir el-Sultan) and the Coptic Patriarchate and is identified by a cross that is painted onto the column.[234]

The Deir el-Sultan (the "Sultan's Monastery") is located on the roof of the Church of the Holy Sepulchre. It sits on the terrace over the Chapel of St. Helena and is involved in a property dispute between the Copts and the Ethiopians. The dispute involves a passageway leading from the Dier el-Sultan to the Chapel of St. Michael and the Chapel of the Angel. The passage made it easy for the Copts to go from St. Anthony's Monastery to their chapel in the rotunda of the Church of the Holy Sepulchre.

The Coptic Church can trace its origins back to St. Mark and has been in the Church of the Holy Sepulchre since the earliest times. The Ethiopian royal dynasty adopted Christianity in the fourth century and became a bishopric of Alexandria. Both the Coptic Church and the Ethiopian Church

---

[233] Zugibe, *The Crucifixion of Jesus*, 46, 48. O'Collins quotes from Seneca's *Epistle 101*, "Can any man be found willing to be fastened to the accursed tree, long sickly, already deformed, swelling with ugly weals on shoulders and chest, and drawing the breath of life amid long-drawn-out agony? He would have many excuses for dying even before mounting the cross." O'Collins, "Crucifixion," *ABD*, 1209. Hengel suggests the "ugly weals on shoulders and chest" mentioned by Seneca were a result of the scourging. Hengel, *Crucifixion*, 30-31.

[234] Salomon and Milner, *Jesus 2000*, 194; Studium Biblicum Franciscanum, "Jerusalem." http://198.62.75.1/www1/ofm/sbf/escurs/Ger/09escursEn.html.

had been in spiritual and dogmatic communion since that time. In 1951, after a long and rigorous campaign for greater autonomy, an Ethiopian was appointed as *abuna* (bishop). As a result of deteriorating relations between President Gamal Abdel Nasser of Egypt and Emperor Haile Selassie of Ethiopia, the two churches broke from each other, and the Ethiopian Church became autocephalous; it was headed by its own primate.[235]

For centuries, the Ethiopians had their own chapels in the Church of the Holy Sepulchre. However, under Ottoman rule, they became poorer, and as a result, they lost their right to the Greeks and became subordinates to the Armenians in the seventeenth century. This was a major dispute with international and political ramifications and dates back to a plague in 1898 that wiped out the local Ethiopian monastic community. When monks were eventually sent to reoccupy their monastery, they were treated as guests by the Coptic patriarchate and were granted permission to pray in the Chapel of the Angel. They were not treated as residents. It is believed that their archives were burned during the plague, and the Ethiopians cannot prove their ownership.

On February 22, 1961, a Jordanian government committee gave ownership of the Deir el-Sultan, the two chapels, and the passageway to the Abyssinians, and the keys were transferred to the Ethiopians. The Egyptian government intervened on April 1. The decision was suspended, and the previous situation was restored. The Copts successfully challenged the decision in the high court, agreeing that the Ethiopians could not prove ownership of the disputed area. The debate continued well into the 1973 October war and beyond. It was finally determined that the governments

---

[235] Cohen, *Saving the Holy Sepulchre*, 193–4.

should not be involved in holy places and could not be relied upon to preserve the Status Quo.[236]

---

[236] Ibid., 194–5, 200–201. There is much discussion on this topic, and it is not the intention of this work to debate the political and spiritual issues. The point is mentioned only to discuss the insistence of the Ethiopians on maintaining a monastery on the roof of the Church of the Holy Sepulchre. For more information, see Raymond Cohen, *Saving the Holy Sepulcher*, 181–200. Recently, the Associated Press reported two incidence of violence at the Church of the Holy Sepulcher. On Palm Sunday, March 23, 2008, Armenian and Greek worshipers came to blows at Christ's tomb. A Greek monk violated the Status Quo that is in place by entering the tomb during an Armenian prayer service. The Armenians "Kicked the Greek monk out of the Edicule." See "Armenian, Greek Worshippers Come to Blows at Jesus' Tomb," *The Associated Press*. http://www.haaretz.com/hasen/spages/976409.html. The Associated Press reported an update to the story on October 11, 2008, when another violent scene occurred. This new incident also involved a violation of the Status Quo when Greek monks blocked the Armenians from continuing with a procession in the Church of the Holy Sepulchre. The feud revolves around the demand by the Greek Orthodox to post a monk inside the Aedicule. One monk had a bloody gash on his forehead. Both monks were taken away in handcuffs. See "Once Again, Monks Come to Blows at Church of Holy Sepulcher," *The Associated Press*. http://haaretz.com/hasen/spages/1035666.html.

The Ninth Station: Jesus Falls For The Third Time

Figure 24: **Left:** The column with the painted cross that separates the Ethiopian rooftop monastery on the left and the Coptic Patriarchate on the right. This marks Station IX where Jesus fell for the third time. **Right:** The cells of the monks living on the roof of the Church of the Holy Sepulchre.[237]

---

[237] Michael L. Russo. Photographed by Michael James Russo, April 23, 2012.

CHAPTER 16

THE TENTH STATION: JESUS IS STRIPPED OF HIS GARMENTS

> *When the soldiers had crucified Jesus, they took His clothes and divided them into four shares, one for each soldier. They also took His tunic, but the tunic was seamless, woven in one piece from the top down. So they said to one another, "Let's not tear it, but cast lots for it to see whose it will be." In order that the passage of Scripture might be fulfilled [that says] "They divided my garments among them, and for my vesture they cast lots." (John 19:23–24)*

𝒮ince Jesus's tunic was woven in one piece, the soldiers must have considered it valuable. Thomas Á Kempis stated, "It was fitting that the robe should remain whole, not only because of the special reverence due it, but it might also proclaim the unity of Holy Mother Church throughout the world."[238] R. Brown reminds us that all four

---

[238] Á Kempis, *On the Passion of Christ*, 89.

The Tenth Station: Jesus Is Stripped Of His Garments

Gospels mention the soldiers dividing Jesus's clothing. He comments that John is careful to demonstrate that the Roman soldiers fulfilled the Scripture "to the nth degree," thus illustrating how Jesus remained in charge.[239] The Gospels of Matthew and Mark support the fact that Jesus did not walk naked to Calvary (Matt. 27:31; Mark 15:20), even though it was the Roman custom to strip the victim to inflict more humiliation. Being sensitive to Jewish customs, Jesus's robe was left on Him during His painful walk.[240] There is debate as to whether Jesus was naked (as was the custom) when He was crucified, and it is not the purpose of this work to enter that debate. As previously referenced, there is evidence that the Romans were sensitive to Jewish customs, for a time, under the reign of Emperor Tiberius.

One can assume that the clothing that Jesus wore was stuck to His body and difficult to remove without causing excruciating pain. We can experience a minor version of this

---

[239] Brown, *An Introduction to the New Testament*, 358.

[240] Zugibe, *The Crucifixion of Jesus*, 48; Barbet, *A Doctor at Calvary*, 55; Janice Bennett, *Sacred Blood, Sacred Image* (Littleton, CO: Libri de Hispania, 2001), 125; Donahue, "Crucifixion," *EDB*, 299. In a letter to Pontius Pilate, Emperor Tiberius wrote, "I have written my prefects elsewhere in the Empire to conciliate the Jews living under their jurisdiction, and not to disturb their established customs. On the contrary, they are not to protect them. The same must certainly apply to the Judean homeland. I herewith charge you to maintain the peace of Judea by disturbing none of the Jewish institutions." This is a paraphrase of Tiberius' sentiments (according to Philo, *De Legatione ad Gaium*, xxiv, 160ff) and referenced by Paul L. Maier, *Pontius Pilate* (Grand Rapids, MI: Kregel Publications, 1968) 170. These exemptions are also cited in Harry W. Tajra, *The Trial of St. Paul* (Tübingen, Germany: Mohr, 1989), 16. Tiberius had been anti-Semitic as seen by his expulsion of the Jews in 19 CE. He may have been influenced by Sejanus, who was anti-Semitic. Once Sejanus died, Tiberius became more favorable to the Jews, and he ordered the governors throughout the empire not to mistreat them. Harold W. Hoener, *Chronological Aspects of the Life of Christ* (Grand Rapids, MI: Zondervan), 1978.

pain ourselves when we have to remove a bandage from a cut or bruise we have received. Typically, some of the threads of the bandage are dried and stuck to the wound, making it painful to remove the dressing. A quick pull removes the bandage, followed by a short but painful feeling as the bandage is torn from the wound. In Jesus's case, His entire body was bloodied from the scourging and the other wounds He received along the route to Calvary. When His clothing was removed from his body, the innumerable nerve endings that were raw and open undoubtedly sent thousands of painful shocks throughout His body. This would be especially true of His back, which had received the brunt of the scourging.[241] Because the Romans had perfected crucifixion to deliver the greatest amount of pain, it is safe to assume that they did not gently remove Jesus's garments. Most likely, they were torn off His body.

Matthew and Mark both state that lots were cast for the garments (Matt. 27:35; Mark 12:24). John is more specific and says the soldiers cast lots for the tunic (John 19:23). The soldiers were used to playing dice games to ease the boredom of a long night's watch. One of the games they liked to play was "*basileus*" (βασιλεύς), which means "king." The game is played by advancing markers according to the throw of the dice. The players race to storm the king's tower, and the winner is the person who gets to the tower first.

---

[241] Barbet, *A Doctor at Calvary*, 166. Gaetner describes the effects of scourging as having one-third of the stripes falling on the front of the person and two-thirds of the stripes falling on the back. See Gaertner, "Scourging," *EDB*, 1173. O'Collins uses an excerpt from Seneca's *Epistle 101* to describe death by crucifixion, including the effects of scourging. O'Collins, "Crucifixion," *ABD*, 1209.

The Tenth Station: Jesus Is Stripped Of His Garments

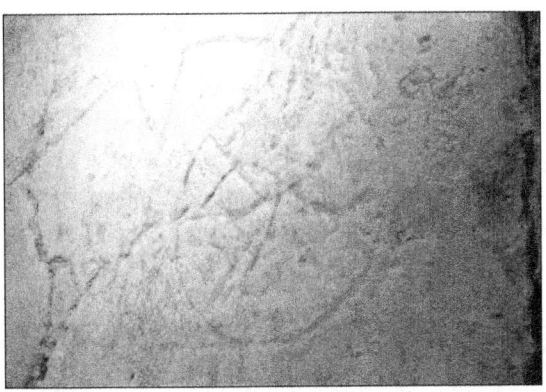

Figure 25. "Basileus" (king) game etched into the pavement at the Lithostrotos. This is a typical game that would be played by Roman soldiers to ease the boredom of long periods of guard duty. Storming the king's tower was the object of the game. The object of the dice game played at the cross was to win Jesus's robe.[242]

The tenth Station of the Cross is in the Chapel of Sorrows. The chapel is known as the Chapel of the Franks and was built by the Crusaders to provide a ceremonial entrance to Calvary. It was closed after the fall of Jerusalem in 1187 and can now only be viewed through the window at Station XI. The room was preserved in its entirety. The entrance to Golgotha was blocked up, and a window was put in its place. Today the chapel is in the hands of the Latin Patriarchate. The chapel is dedicated to the Blessed Virgin Mary and John the Baptist.[243] According to J. Abela, OFM, the commemoration of Jesus's being stripped of His garments only appeared in Jerusalem at a late period. Although he does not provide a specific date, he believes the stripping mentioned by the

---

[242] Michael L. Russo. Photographed by Michael James Russo, April 25, 2012. The dice game reminds people of the soldiers casting lots at the foot of the cross.

[243] Salomon and Milner, *Jesus 2000*, 196; Adrian J. Boas, *Jerusalem in the Time of the Crusades* (New York, NY: Routledge, 2001), 108; Murphy-O'Connor, *The Holy Land*, 50–52.

Anglo-Saxon pilgrim Saewulf in 1102–1103 is associated with the crowning of thorns and of Christ's being mocked and insulted. In those days, the crowning with thorns and mocking were memorialized at the foot of Calvary. Today, when you enter the main door of the Church of the Holy Sepulchre, a stairway on the right takes you to a spot where Jesus faced the death sentence.[244]

Figure 26. **Left:** The courtyard of the Chapel of the Franks where Jesus's being stripped of his garments is commemorated. The altar inside the chapel is dedicated to the Blessed Virgin Mary and John the Baptist. **Right:** The stairway inside the Church that leads to Golgotha, the place of the crucifixion. [245]

---

[244] John Abela, OFM, and Michael Olteanu, Franciscan Cyberspot-Christusrex 1998, "Jerusalem, The Way of the Cross, Via Crucis. http://www.christusrex.org /www1/jsc?TVCstatn10.html.

[245] Left: Michael L. Russo. Photographed by Michael James Russo, April 28, 2012. Right: Todd Bolen/BiblePlaces.com, Church of the Holy Sepulchre, stairs to place of crucifixion, adr080719438.

CHAPTER 17

THE ELEVENTH STATION: JESUS IS NAILED TO THE CROSS

As dry as a potsherd is my throat; my tongue sticks to my palate; you lay me in the dust of death. Many dogs surround me; a pack of evil doers closes in on me. So wasted are my hands and feet that I can count all my bones. They stare at me and gloat. (Ps. 22:16–18)

The cross that was waiting for Jesus was just one of several on Golgotha. It would have been of medium height and in the form of a T, the *crux commissa*. According to the opinion of archaeologists, the *crux commissa* was the normal form of a Roman cross.[246] Considering what we have learned concerning the history and practice of Roman-style crucifixion, the Gospel accounts provide a sanitized ver-

---

[246] Barbet, *A Doctor at Calvary*, 177; O'Collins, "Crucifixion," *ABD*, 1208; Donahue, "Crucifixion," *EDB*, 298; Edwards, and others, "The Physical Death of Jesus Christ."

sion of the event.²⁴⁷ As referenced in the introduction of this book, prior to 1950s, the lack of definitive information concerning the practice of crucifixion left both clergy and laity with insufficient knowledge for preparing meaningful homilies, sermons, and programs that present an accurate picture of Christ's Passion and death.

Jehohanan, the son of HGQWL, referenced in chapter 7 of this book, was nailed to the cross through his forearms.²⁴⁸ Scripture tells us that Jesus was not nailed through the forearms but through the hands and feet (cf. Luke 24:38–40; cf. John 20:20). The story of Thomas, the doubter, makes it clear that Jesus was not crucified like Jehohanan (cf. John 20:24–29). However, there is debate as to the actual positioning of the nails and the number of nails used. Christian art has added to this confusion by depicting Jesus on the cross in a variety of ways.

---

[247] Regis Martin, *Suffering of Love*, 86.

[248] Holloway, *A Death in Jerusalem*, 67. J. Zias disagrees and states that most crucifixion victims were tied to the cross. However, he admits that Martin Hengel, who has written "the most definitive scholarly report on crucifixion antiquity," states that the victim was always nailed to the cross and tying the victim was the exception.

The Eleventh Station: Jesus Is Nailed To The Cross

Figure 27. **Left:** Artist Nikolai Ge depicts Jesus being nailed through the wrist and through the ankles. This painting hangs in the Musée d'Orsay in Paris, France. **Right:** Artist Josse Lieferinxe depicts Jesus being nailed through the hands with one nail through His feet. His painting also suggests the use of a *suppadenum*, or foot rest.[249]

Jesus would have been extremely exhausted when He arrived at Calvary. It is plausible that He was in a moderate state of traumatic shock and *hypovolemic* shock. His shoulders would have been traumatized from carrying the *patibulum*, and it is possible He suffered from a collapsed lung due to the scourging. Dehydration would have exacerbated His weakened condition, and fluid would have continued to collect around His lungs, making it increasingly difficult to breathe.[250]

---

[249] Left photo: Public domain; Nikolai Ge, www.wikipaintings.org/en/nikolai-ge/not_detected_252986. Right photo: Public domain; Josse Lieferinxe, www.bing.com/images/search?q=josse+lieferinxe+public-+domain&view=detail&id=8FAE349DA01F51CF0119348744BA69440C36D4CF.

[250] *Hypovolemic* shock is a condition due to a severe injury in which the body has lost so much blood volume that there is not enough

When the executioners were ready, they threw Jesus to the ground. He was forced to lie on His back while His shoulders were placed on the rough surface of the *patibulum*. His arms were stretched out, ready to be nailed. The rest of His body, already bloodied and clotted with scabs, gathered dust and gravel as it was moved into position by the soldiers.[251] While He was being held in place, each arm was stretched out parallel to the *patibulum*, and a large spikelike nail was nailed through His wrist just below the bulge at the base of the thumb. The pain would have been excruciating, causing Jesus to cry out. However, P. Barbet states that Jesus did not cry out, even though he admits that the nail hit the median nerve causing inexpressible pain.[252] His definitive admission is interesting because he was not present. One can speculate that Barbet formed his opinion from Sacred Scripture because the writers are silent on this matter. F. Zugibe agrees with the seriousness of the pain and disagrees with

---

blood to circulate throughout the body to deliver sufficient oxygen to the vital organs. Zugibe, *The Crucifixion of Jesus*, 15, 25, 49, 132, 135. Hengel agrees that Jesus was extremely weakened from the flogging and from carrying of the *patibulum*. Hengel, *Crucifixion*, 32.

[251] Barbet, *A Doctor at Calvary*, 167; Zugibe, *The Crucifixion of Jesus*, 65–66. The descriptions of crucifixion provided by O'Collins and Donahue can be used to support the findings of both Zugibe and Barbet. Although they do not specifically address this particular issue, one can easily envision the rough treatment used by the Roman soldiers. See also *Crucifixion*, DVD, A&E Networks; *The Crucifixion of Christ, A Return to the Cross*, DVD, Bema Publishing; *How Jesus Died, the Final 18 Hours*, DVD, Trinity Pictures; O'Collins, "Crucifixion," *ABD*, 1207–1208; Donahue, "Crucifixion," *EDB*, 298–299; Edwards, and others, "The Physical Death of Jesus Christ." Hengel's book, *Crucifixion*, provides additional details concerning crucifixion in antiquity.

[252] Barbet, *A Doctor at Calvary*, 167. The descriptions presented by Hengel, O'Collins, and Donahue attest to the excruciating pain experienced by the victim being crucified. Barbet's comments concerning Jesus's silence during the nailing are his opinion.

Barbet. Zugibe adds, "The pain would have been brutal, like hot pokers traversing His arms like lightning bolts, causing Jesus to arch His torso and let out piercing screams."[253]

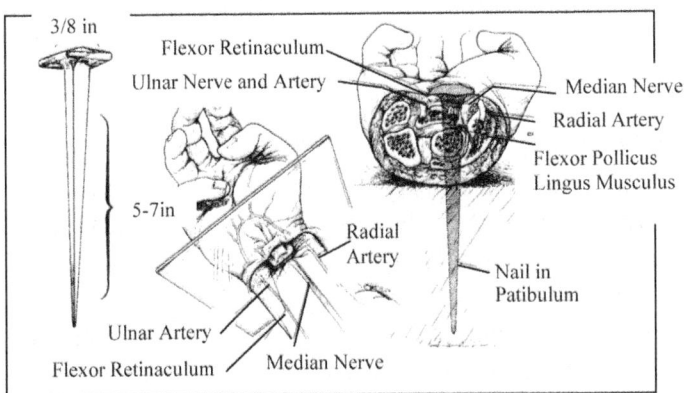

Figure 28. The nailing of the wrists. **Left:** The size of iron nail. **Center:** The location of the nail in the wrist, between *carpals* and *radius*. **Right:** A cross-section view of the wrist, at a level of plane indicated at the left, showing the path of the nail, with the probable transection of the median nerve and impalement of *flexor pollicis longus*, but without injury to major arterial trunks and without the fracturing of bones.[254]

Zugibe and Barbet disagree on the position of the nails. Barbet's experiments concluded that Jesus was nailed through the wrists. He claims that if nailed through the palms, the hand can only support for a short time, approximately one hundred pounds. The pressure of the victim's weight dragging down would cause the hand to quickly rip free. Barbet emphatically states, "Crucifixion was not through the palms

---

[253] Zugibe, *The Crucifixion of Jesus*, 66. Given the descriptions by Hengel, O'Collins, Donahue, De la Potterie, and others, it is believable that Jesus, in His humanity, would have screamed out in pain.

[254] Edwards, and others, "The Physical Death of Jesus Christ."

of the hands but through the wrists."[255] Zugibe questions the accuracy of Barbet's research and defends his own findings that individuals weighing up to two hundred and twenty-five pounds can be nailed through the palms at sixty-five degree angles. He claims that tearing would not occur if both feet are secured to the upright (*stipes*) section of the cross.[256] Barbet is open to challenge and criticism and states, "I can claim that since I finished my experiments the conclusions to which I came have never been reversed, though I remain open to new discovery which may show me to have been wrong."[257] Interestingly, Padre Pio (St. Pio of Pietrelcina) was asked why his hand wounds were not in the wrists where victims of crucifixion were routinely nailed; he shrugged his shoulders and said, "Oh, I guess it would be too much to have them exactly like they were in the case of Our Lord."[258]

Sacred Scripture is also not specific on this point. The Gospels only speak of hands and do not mention palms or wrists. When one considers that Barbet states that the hand consists of the wrist, *metacarpus*, and the fingers,[259] one realizes that the position of the nails can be debated indefinitely. Both men do agree that the nails did hit the median nerve,

---

[255] Barbet, *A Doctor at Calvary*, 47. Barbet's experiment can be found on pp. 92–105. For additional commentary, see *Crucifixion*, DVD, A&E Networks; *The Crucifixion of Christ, A Return to the Cross*, DVD, Bema Publishing, *How Jesus Died, the Final 18 Hours*, DVD, Trinity Pictures; Hengel, *Crucifixion*, 25, 31.

[256] The complete study can be found in Zugibe, *The Crucifixion of Jesus*, 65–95. Hengel states that the victims were nailed by both hands and feet and does not comment about the practice of nailing through the wrist. Hengel, 31. See Edwards, and others, "The Physical Death of Jesus Christ."

[257] Barbet, *A Doctor at Calvary*, 9.

[258] C. Bernard Ruffin, *Padre Pio: The True Story* (Huntington, IN: Our Sunday Visitor Publishing Division, 1991), 165.

[259] Barbet, *A Doctor at Calvary*, 94.

The Eleventh Station: Jesus Is Nailed To The Cross

and Zugibe does concede that driving the nail through the wrist cannot be excluded as a possible pathway.[260] Among the many theories is the sedile theory. The sedile theory suggests the use of a saddle on the cross (*sedile*). The saddle would support the weight of the body, which would otherwise tear itself away from the nails that were driven through the hands. The use of the saddle prolonged the torture and agony.[261] There is no concrete evidence that a saddle was used in Jesus's crucifixion, and both Zugibe and Barbet reject the sedile theory. Zugibe states that the Passover and Sabbath were too close; therefore, a procedure would not be used that would prolong Jesus's life. Barbet states that the cross awaiting Jesus would have been the normal Roman cross.[262]

Once Jesus was nailed to the *patibulum*, it was time to lift Him onto the *stipes*. The Gospels do not provide any information as to the exact method used to raise Jesus on the cross. The soldiers probably followed the regular Roman custom. The upright *stipes* remained fixed in the ground. The *patibulum* was then affixed to it using ropes, and Jesus was hoisted up so that the *patibulum* could be affixed to the *stipes*.[263] Four men could easily perform this task if the cross was between six and eight feet high. A small ladder could be placed against the *stipes*, and the victim could be lifted backward up the ladder so that *patibulum* could be affixed to

---

[260] Zugibe, *The Crucifixion of Jesus*, 78.

[261] Holloway, *A Death in Jerusalem*, 66; O'Collins, "Crucifixion," *ABD*, 1209; Donahue, "Crucifixion," *EDB*, 298; Hengel, *Crucifixion*, 25; Barbet, *A Doctor at Calvary*, 45; Zugibe, *Crucifixion of Jesus*, 57, 59,

[262] Zugibe, *The Crucifixion of Jesus*, 59; Barbet, *A Doctor at Calvary*, 60. This view is also held by O'Collins, Hengel, and others because this was the Roman custom.

[263] R. Brown and others, "The Life of Jesus of Nazareth," in *BTBA*, 442; O'Collins, "Crucifixion," *ABD*, 1209; Barbet, *A Doctor at Calvary*, 50, 100.

the *stipes*. If the cross was higher, this still could have been accomplished with little extra effort.

Most crosses were short (*humilis*). This allowed the dogs and other predatory animals to easily attack the crucified victim once the crowds and the guards left the area. This added to the horror and humiliation of crucifixion. Short crosses also simplified the work for the executioners because they were usually pressed for time due to the many crucifixions that were scheduled. Because crucifixions were performed almost daily in Jerusalem, convenience was an important issue for those who had to carry them out. This method of lifting the *patibulum* is the only solution that agrees with what we have learned from archaeology.[264] In John 3:14, Jesus states, "And just as Moses lifted up the serpent in the desert, so must the Son of Man be lifted up, so that everyone who believes in Him may have eternal life." He teaches in John 8:28, "When you lift up the Son of Man, then you will realize that 'I AM.'" In John 12:32–33, Jesus again speaks about being lifted up: "And when I am lifted up from the earth, I will draw everyone to myself." John 12:33 continues by telling us, "He said this indicating the kind of death He would die."

Once Jesus was raised up on the cross, the soldiers nailed His feet to the *stipes*. The exact manner in which His feet were nailed to the cross is still being debated. Christian art depicts Jesus's feet being nailed either one on top of the other or both nailed separately. Citing their own research, both Zugibe and Barbet suggest that there was no supporting platform (*suppedaneum*) for His feet. They allege His feet were nailed directly to the *stipes*. When one considers the large number of crucifixions that were being performed daily, it does seem natural that each foot would have been

---

[264] Barbet, *A Doctor at Calvary*, 56; Edwards, and others, "The Physical Death of Jesus Christ."

The Eleventh Station: Jesus Is Nailed To The Cross

nailed separately simply because it would have been easier and faster. The bones would be less likely to break in this way, and this method also coincides with the tradition found in early Christian references. The artistic depictions that show one foot being nailed on top of another did not begin to surface until the early eleventh century.

Although the Shroud of Turin is used as proof that the feet were nailed on top of each other, it is impossible to make a determination as to the actual position of the feet on the cross. However, it was common to nail the feet by bending the knees and sliding the soles of the feet up the *stipes* so that the soles would lie flat. This would create a similar situation to that of the hands. That is, the nail would rub against the plantar nerve in the foot just like it would rub against the median nerve in the wrist, and the maximum amount of pain would be felt by the victim.[265] By nailing the feet flat to the *stipes*, there would not be a shelf or platform for the victim to use for rest.

---

[265] Barbet, *A Doctor at Calvary*, 177; Details of Zugibe's experiment can be found in Zugibe, *The Crucifixion of Jesus*, 66–99, specific details can be found on pages 95–99. In addition, see Edwards and others, "The Physical Death of Jesus Christ; *Crucifixion*, DVD, A&E Networks; *The Crucifixion of Christ, A Return to the Cross*, DVD, Bema Publishing; *How Jesus Died, the Final 18 Hours*, DVD, Trinity Pictures. Hengel advises that all attempts to provide a perfect description of crucifixion are in vain because the executioners were given full rein to use any one of a variety of sadistic methods. Hengel, *Crucifixion*, 24–25.

The Via Dolorosa

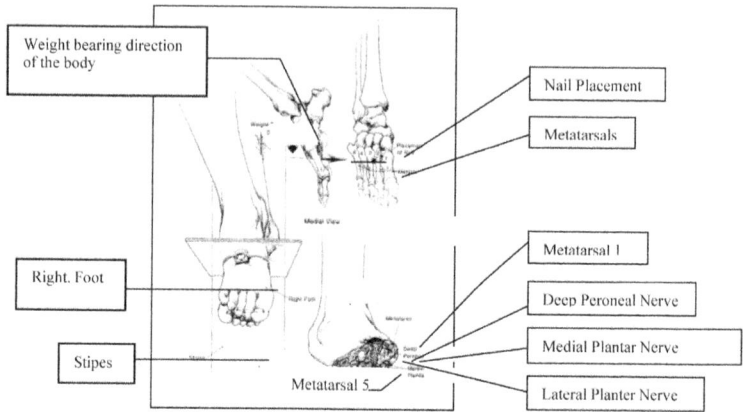

Figure 29. The nailing of the feet. **Left:** The position of feet atop one another and against the *stipes*. **Upper Right:** The location of the nail in the second *intermetatarsal* space. **Lower Right:** A cross section of a foot showing the path of the nail.[266]

After a short period of time, severe cramps, numbness, and coldness in the thighs caused by the compression of the bent knees would have forced Jesus to arch His back and attempt to lift Himself up so He could straighten His knees and relieve the pain. This would continue for the entire time that Jesus was on the cross. The pain Jesus was experiencing would have been unrelenting and affected His entire body. His pain would have been increased by everything around Him, including the air blowing over His raw skin, which was sensitive due to nerve damage, the pressure of the nails in constant contact with the median and plantar nerves, and the movements of His body.[267]

---

[266] Edwards, and others, "The Physical Death of Jesus Christ;" Holloway, *A Death in Jerusalem*, 67–68; *Crucifixion*, DVD, A&E Networks; *The Crucifixion of Christ, A Return to the Cross*, DVD, Bema Publishing; *How Jesus Died, the Final 18 Hours*, DVD, Trinity Pictures.

[267] Pixner, *With Jesus in Jerusalem*, 141–142; Zugibe, *The Crucifixion of Jesus*, 131–135; Barbet, *A Doctor at Calvary*, 76–77; *Crucifixion*, DVD, A&E Networks; *The Crucifixion of Christ, A Return to the*

The Eleventh Station: Jesus Is Nailed To The Cross

Figure 30. By the seventeenth century, artists tended to dispense with the crowds of figures (saints, centurions, onlookers) who had almost dominated the earlier compositions. This oil painting on wood, by Peter Paul Rubens, depicts a solitary figure of Christ against a darkened background. His hands are nailed at the wrist, and His feet are nailed one on top of the other and are flat against the *stipes*.[268]

In an effort to communicate respect for Jesus, yet still convey the horrors of crucifixion, artists throughout the centuries have depicted Jesus in various positions on the cross. None, however, convey the true horror of crucifixion.

Today, Golgotha in the Church of the Holy Sepulchre is divided into two main chapels. The chapel at Station XI belongs to the Latin Patriarchate, and the chapel at Station XII belongs to the Greek Orthodox. Station XIII lies between these two Stations and is under the care of the Franciscans. Golgotha has been called the "navel of the world" because it is both the traditional site of the "binding of Isaac" and the

---

Cross, DVD, Bema Publishing; *How Jesus Died, the Final 18 Hours*, DVD, Trinity Pictures.

[268] Public domain.

The Via Dolorosa

locus of the crucifixion. "It is here that Adam was created from dust and here that his skull is buried."[269]

The silver altar that is at Station XI was donated in 1588 by the Duke (Cardinal) of Medici from Tuscany. The altar was made in Florence. The four scenes depicted in the altar are associated with the Passion and death of Jesus and are hammered in silver.[270]

Figure 31. A mosaic depicting Jesus's being nailed to the cross hangs over the altar at Station XI. Standing above Jesus is His mother, Mary, and John. Four scenes commemorating the Passion and death of Christ are carved in silver in the front of the altar.[271]

---

[269] Salomon and Milner, *Jesus 2000*, 196. Reference is made to Jerusalem being the navel of the world in Michael D. Coogan, *The Old Testament* (New York, NY: Oxford University Press, 2006), 397.

[270] Salomon and Milner, *Jesus 2000*, 196; Holy Land Photos, "Medici Altar." http://www.holylandphotos.org/browse.asp?s=1,2,6,19,321,323&img=IJNTHSCL03.

[271] Michael L. Russo. Photographed by Michael James Russo, April 23, 2012.

The Eleventh Station: Jesus Is Nailed To The Cross

Pope Benedict XVI has said,

> The cross ... is the definitive "sign" par excellence given to us so that we might understand the truth about man and about God: we have all been created and redeemed by a God who sacrificed his only Son out of love. This is why the crucifixion ... "is the culmination of that turning of God against himself in which he gives himself in order to raise man up and save him. This is love in its most radical form." (*Deus Caritas Est*, no.12)[272]

---

[272] Homily at the Roman parish Dio Padre Misericordioso given by Pope Benedict XVI, March 26, 2006. Benedict XVI, *Spiritual Thoughts* (Canada: USCCB Publishing, 2007), 122.

CHAPTER 18

THE TWELFTH STATION: JESUS DIES ON THE CROSS

Jesus cried out in a loud voice, "Father, into your hands I commend my spirit;" and when He had said this He breathed His last. (Luke 23:46)

We have identified a long list of circumstances and causes for Jesus's dying so quickly. These include His mental agony, His physical condition,[273] His knowledge of all the sins of men, and the burden that He was assuming for their redemption. Given all of the events leading up to Christ's death, the speed of His passing should not surprise us. The scourging was enough to kill Him. The journey to Calvary, the wounds from the nails, and the heartbreak and

---

[273] Barbet, *A Doctor at Calvary*, 69; O'Collins provides a thorough description of the crucifixion of Christ in "Crucifixion," *ABD*, 1207-1210. See *Crucifixion*, DVD, A&E Networks; *The Crucifixion of Christ, A Return to the Cross*, DVD, Bema Publishing; *How Jesus Died, the Final 18 Hours*, DVD, Trinity Pictures; Edwards, and others, "The Physical Death of Jesus Christ."

The Twelfth Station: Jesus Dies On The Cross

fatigue were more than sufficient to account for His rapid death.[274]

The Gospel accounts agree that Jesus died on a Friday, the day of preparation for the Sabbath. According to Mark 15:25, Jesus was crucified at 9:00 AM, the third hour. He died at 3:00 PM, the ninth hour. Jesus spent six hours on the cross, which was a relatively short period of time. It was not unusual for a victim to last a few days before dying.[275] Again, the Gospels speak of the crucifixion as a general cause of Christ's death, and this leaves many unanswered questions. Did He succumb to heart failure, extreme loss of body fluids, asphyxiation, or other factors? Was it a combination of everything that He had suffered? There are even some who believe Jesus did not die on the cross but was alive when He was taken down. This concept, known as the swoon theory, asserts that Jesus was either unconscious or in a coma when He was taken down from the cross. This theory is embraced by those who wish to deny the resurrection. Karl Bahrdt, in his work, *Auführung des Plans und Zwecks Jesu (1784–1792)*, proposed that Jesus was a member of the secret order of Essenes and was treated with drugs by Luke to help Him endure the crucifixion. A similar story was circulated by Karl Venturini. Venturini added that a member of the secret society dressed in a white beard moaned from the tomb and frightened the guards. Once the guards fled, the

---

[274] Holloway, *A Death in Jerusalem*, 69; Hengel, *Crucifixion*, 28–29, 31–32

[275] R. Brown and others, "The Life of Jesus of Nazareth," in *BTBA*, 445; O'Collins provides a thorough description of the crucifixion of Christ. See *Crucifixion*, DVD, A&E Networks; *The Crucifixion of Christ, A Return to the Cross*, DVD, Bema Publishing; *How Jesus Died, the Final 18 Hours* DVD, Trinity Pictures.

The Via Dolorosa

bearded character rescued Christ from the tomb, and Jesus went to live in seclusion.[276]

In 1894, Nicolas Notovich, a Russian war correspondent, reported in his book, *La vie inconnue de Jésus-Christ*, that following an accident, he (Notovich) was taken to the Himis Lama Monastery in Tibet. The monks of that monastery worshipped a prophet named Issa (supposedly Jesus). Notovich reported that documents existed proving Jesus traveled to Tibet during His "lost years" (the years between Jesus's youth and His ministry) and learned Buddhism and other religious sects.[277] Notovich's publication was translated into at least four languages and was published throughout Europe and America.[278] The list of skeptics goes on.

One of the most recent theories was published by Kjell Ytrehus, a Norwegian physician. In 2002, Ytrehus stated that Jesus appeared to be dead but was actually in a coma due to hypothermia. The hypothermia was attributed to unseasonably cool weather, and Ytrehus indicated that Christ was "a probable victim of a cool-down." He adds that Jesus was laid in a cave and not buried because Pontius Pilate probably accepted a bribe to permit Jesus to be taken off the cross so

---

[276] G. Habermas discusses the various theories that were presented concerning the swoon theory in Gary R. Habermas, *The Risen Jesus and Future Hope* (Lanham, MD: Rowman & Littlefield Publishers, Inc., 2003), 13–15.

[277] Nicholas Notovich, *The Unknown Life of Jesus Christ* (New York, NY: R.F. Fenno Company, 1890), 164–218. This book is in the public domain and has been reprinted by Kessinger Publishing, Whitefish, MT: 2004. The "Life of St. Issa (who is supposed to be Jesus Christ) is described on pages 164–218.

[278] P. Jenkins supplies additional information concerning K. Bahrdt, K. Venturini, N. Notovich, and others in Philip Jenkins, *Hidden Gospels* (New York, NY: Oxford University Press, 2001), 47–53.

soon. None of these stories have any scientific, theological, or historic support.[279]

P. Kreeft and R. Tacelli provide arguments for refuting the swoon theory. The most obvious arguments they present begin with the fact that Jesus was in very grave physical condition. Second, the soldiers were sure Jesus was dead and did not break His legs, as was the custom. As an eyewitness, John saw blood and water come from Christ's side when the spear pierced it. Jesus's body was wrapped in burial linen and laid in the tomb. A swooning Jesus would not have been able to roll back the stone from the entrance of the tomb and certainly would not have been able to overcome the guards.[280] The Scriptures tell us that Jesus appeared to Mary Magdalene and walked with His disciples on the road to Emmaus on the Sunday after He was crucified. Given the condition of His body and the fact that His feet had been nailed to the cross, a swooning Jesus would have taken a long period of time to gather enough strength to walk and would have needed considerable time before His wounds were healed enough for Him to walk or even stand.[281]

---

[279] Kjell Ytrehus, "Jesus Was Dead after Crucifixion?" *Tidsskrift for Den norske legeforening*, vol. 122, no. 8 (March, 2002), 833. http://www. tidsskriftet.no/? seks_id=526889. Zugibe, *The Crucifixion of Jesus*, 145–160; John Dominic Crossan and N. T. Wright, *The Resurrection of Jesus* (Minneapolis; MN, 2005), 84; Gary R. Habermas, *The Risen Jesus and Future Hope*, 13–15; Philip Jenkins, *Hidden Gospels*, 47–53. Raymond Brown discusses the various attacks made against the death of Christ. See Raymond Brown, "The Resurrection of Jesus," in *NJBC*, §81:121–126, 1373–75.

[280] Peter Kreeft and Ronald K. Tacelli, *Handbook of Christian Apologetics* (Downers Grove, IL: InterVarsity Press, 1994), 183–184.

[281] Zugibe, *The Crucifixion of Jesus*, 162. For additional information concerning the swoon theory, see Gary R. Habermas, *The Historical Jesus* (Joplin, MO: College Press Publishing Company, 1996), 75–99; Habermas, *The Risen Jesus and Future Hope*, 3–51. The entire first chapter discusses the issues surrounding the swoon theory and refutes

There are many theories concerning the cause of Christ's death. Rather than present a list of possibilities, F. Zugibe and P. Barbet focus on the most reasonable and credible. According to both men, the causes that deserve attention are asphyxiation, heart-related causes, and shock. The most widely discussed is asphyxiation. F. Zugibe conducted extensive experiments and concluded that the cause of death was cardiac and respiratory arrest due to hypovolemic and traumatic shock.[282] Other reports suggest similar findings.[283] P. Barbet emphatically states, "All the crucified died of asphyxia."[284] Barbet offers an extensive discussion of the struggle experienced by the victim. During crucifixion, the body sags considerably, and it becomes increasingly difficult for the victim to breath. He or she must keep pushing up to allow the lungs to fill with air. Because the feet are nailed flat to the *stipes*, it is difficult and painful to keep a comfortable rhythm of straightening the body and relaxing it so that the victim can breathe. An exhausted victim such as Jesus could not have kept this up for a long period of time. Once the victim had decided that the struggle was too difficult, he or she gave up and succumbed to death quickly.[285]

---

the theory with Scripture and commentary from theologians such as Raymond Brown.

[282] The documented experiment can be found in Zugibe, *The Crucifixion of Jesus*, 129–136. See *Crucifixion*, DVD, A&E Networks; *The Crucifixion of Christ, A Return to the Cross*, DVD, Bema Publishing; *How Jesus Died, the Final 18 Hours*, DVD.

[283] Edwards, and others, "The Physical Death of Jesus Christ."

[284] Barbet, *A Doctor at Calvary*, 74, 76; O'Collins, "Crucifixion," *ABD*, 1209; *Crucifixion*, DVD, A&E Networks; *The Crucifixion of Christ, A Return to the Cross*, DVD, Bema Publishing; *How Jesus Died, the Final 18 Hours*, DVD, Trinity Pictures; Edwards, and others, "The Physical Death of Jesus Christ."

[285] Barbet, *A Doctor at Calvary*, 74–77.

The Twelfth Station: Jesus Dies On The Cross

The Synoptic Gospels state that Jesus let out a loud cry before dying (Matt. 27:50; Mark 15:37; Luke 23:46). William Stroud used these references to support his theory that Jesus suffered some type of heart rupture or failure. He also relied on John 19:34.[286] Zugibe, citing his own forensic pathology credentials and experience, rejects any reference to Jesus's suffering a heart attack or a ruptured heart.[287] According to Zugibe, because Jesus was only thirty-three years old, it was unlikely that he suffered a heart attack. Although heart attacks can strike young victims, his experience has shown that a person in the younger age group would most likely suffer a heart attack due to diet, lack of exercise, or other "luxuries of civilization." His research suggests that atherosclerosis and myocardial infarctions (heart attacks) were extremely rare in that region of the world at Jesus's time. In addition, he believes that because Jesus was on the cross for such a short period of time, it would have taken at least twenty-four hours for the heart muscle to soften enough to rupture. The exact medical cause of Jesus's death and the condition of His heart are still being debated. The discussions tie to another debate: did Jesus actually die on the cross? This is not a debate to be discussed or decided in this book.

From the Synoptic Gospels, one gets the feeling that it is finally over. Jesus has felt the emptiness of abandonment, cried out to the Father, and died. John presents a different picture. According to I. De La Potterie, the Jesus represented in John's Gospel is anything but a broken man. Jesus dominates the events. He is the one in charge. He is the master

---

[286] William Stroud provides an extensive explanation for his support of the ruptured heart theory. See William Stroud, MD, *The Physical Cause of the Death of Christ* (New York, NY: D. Appleton and Company, 1871), 85-156; Zugibe, *The Crucifixion of Jesus*, 123.

[287] Zugibe served as the director of Cardiovascular Research with the U.S. Veterans Administration in Pittsburgh and as a fellow of the American College of Cardiology.

The Via Dolorosa

of the situation, and it is He who takes the initiative. Of His own free will, He meets His accusers.[288]

Whether Jesus died from asphyxiation or heart trauma compounded by traumatic shock will continue to be debated. The actual fact is that we really do not know the specific cause of His death; we do not have a coroner's report from Jesus's actual crucifixion. The experiments and studies conducted by F. Zugibe, P. Barbet, and others give us an idea of what could have been, and it is from these reports that we can form various opinions. However, whatever the medical reason, Jesus did give us some clues concerning His own death. In John's Gospel, Jesus says about His life, "No one takes it from me, but I lay it down on my own. I have the power to lay it down, and the power to take it up again. This command I have received from my Father (John 10:18)." Jesus died at the hour that He decided. He remained in control until He decided give up His Spirit (Matt. 27:50; Mark 15:37; Luke 23:46; John 19:30).

Both Matthew and Mark tell us that Jesus cried out at the ninth hour, "My God, My God, why have you forsaken me?" (Matt: 27:46; Mark 15:34). The bystanders did not realize that Jesus was calling God (the word for addressing God is *Eli*) and thought He was calling Elijah.[289] This cry is viewed as a feeling of total abandonment. In reality, Jesus was probably praying Psalm 22, which begins with the words "My God, my God, why have you abandoned me?" Prayer was central to who Jesus was. Sacred Scripture frequently tells us that Jesus went off to pray. It would not be uncommon for Him to lift His voice in prayer to the Father when He felt most abandoned. Unlike Mathew and Mark who speak of a

---

[288] Zugibe, *The Crucifixion of Jesus*, 126-7; De la Potterie, *The Hour of Jesus*, 29.

[289] R. Brown and others, "The Life of Jesus of Nazareth," in *BTBA*, 444.

The Twelfth Station: Jesus Dies On The Cross

prayer of anguish, John tells us it is a cry of accomplishment. The goal had been achieved, the end had been accomplished, and the will of the Father had been fulfilled. R. Holloway states, "The death of Jesus was not a despairing act of self-destruction; it was a gift to His friends."[290]

To understand Jesus's prayer to the Father, one must examine the context of Psalm 22:1–32. B. Anderson, Professor Emeritus of Old Testament Theology at Princeton Theological Seminary, provides commentary for each strophe of Psalm 22. According to Anderson, the beginning of the psalm is a cry of distress (Psalm 22:1–3):

My God, My God, why have you abandoned me?
Why so far from my call for help,
from my cries of anguish?
My God I call by day, but you do not answer;
by night but I have no relief.

The cry of distress then turns to an expression of trust (Psalm 22:4–6) and then to one of lament (Psalm 22: 7–9). The lament transforms into a prayer of confidence (Psalm 22:10–11) before becoming a petition for help and a further description of distress (Psalm 22:12–19). In verses 20–22, the petition for help is renewed before turning into a vow of praise and thanksgiving (Psalm 22:23–27). The psalm continues and ends in renewed thanksgiving (Psalm 22:28–32).

> As can be seen from the overall pattern, these cries out of the depths of distress are motivated by a deep confidence that *YHWH* is the compassionate God—the God who hears, who is concerned, and who is involved with the people. The God whom Israel worships is not character-

---

[290] Holloway, *A Death in Jerusalem*, 73, 77.

ized by apathy, but by *pathos*—a sensitivity to the human condition.[291]

Regarding Psalm 22, Benedict Janecko, OSB, states in *The Psalms, Heartbeat of Life and Worship*:

> (Psalm 22) characterizes the structure of laments in that verses 2 to 22 make known the cry, the lament, and the plea for help, while the end of the psalm (verses 23–32) concludes on a note of confidence as do most laments. The very structure then, lends itself to a passion/death/resurrection model.[292]

The prayer that opens with the heart-wrenching feeling of being abandoned by God ends on a note of hope. When Jesus finished praying the psalm, He ended with the words, "Father, into your hands I commend my spirit" (Luke 23:46).[293] In my opinion, this is a perfect example of Jesus's being in control. He lifted His voice to the Father in the Garden of Gethsemane. In anguish He cried out for divine assistance. He accepted the will of the Father, and His journey to the cross began. Now, on the cross, He raised His voice to the Father. He began with cries of distress and lament and ended with words of praise and hope. He decided when He would give up His Spirit (John 10:18), but only after He turned to the Father in prayer. The beauty of this moment is His gift of life to us.

One needs to be careful when reflecting on the Passion and death of Jesus not to let the true meaning of the cross get overshadowed by the horrors of Christ's sufferings.

---

[291] Anderson, *Out of the Depths*, 65.

[292] Benedict Janecko, OSB, *The Psalms, Heartbeat of Life and Worship* (St. Meinrad, IN: St. Meinrad Archabbey, 1995), 35.

[293] Pixner, *With Jesus in Jerusalem*, 143, 146.

The Twelfth Station: Jesus Dies On The Cross

Reflecting on the details of Christ's Passion and death provides a forum for understanding the gift of God's love and the importance of Christ's mission. He suffered rejection and betrayal. He was deserted and denied by His friends. People told lies about Him, hated Him, and deceived Him. Jesus knew what it was like to suffer all aspects of pain. He had His heart broken, He suffered unspeakable physical pain, and He was betrayed and felt abandoned. Therefore, He understands all of our sufferings—all of our daily crosses.[294] As G. Rooney puts it:

> The Prince of Darkness tried to put out the Light of the World! Satan was permitted to smash and bruise the Sacred Body of Our Lord. But when he had done his worst he found that instead of putting out the Light of the World he had only succeeded in helping to light a more brilliant flame!
>
> From Christ's broken heart, God's *Wisdom* and *Power* and *Love* rushed forth, outward and upward and onward, filling the heavens and earth, increasing every moment to the end of time; giving hope where before had been despair; joy where before had been sorrow; life where before there had been death. Here is the real meaning of God's expanding universe of Goodness.[295]

The Price of Darkness failed to put out the Light of the World. The Light of the World was never as bright as it was on that first Good Friday when it beamed throughout the world from the throne of the cross.

As previously mentioned, there are five Stations of the Cross located inside the Church of the Holy Sepulchre. Golgotha, the place of the crucifixion, and Christ's tomb are

---

[294] Rooney, *The Mystery of Calvary*, 87.
[295] Ibid., 89.

The Via Dolorosa

located in the same general area.[296] Once inside the church, visitors use the staircase located on the right that leads up to the traditional site of Golgotha. The rock of Golgotha is enclosed in a Plexiglas case to protect it.[297]

Figure 32. Golgotha is protected by a glass enclosure.[298]

The altar in the chapel commemorating the crucifixion is under Greek Orthodox care. Beneath the altar is a silver disk marking the spot where the cross was placed. There are two additional disks on either side of the altar that mark the area where the two thieves were crucified alongside Jesus. To the

---

[296] Wilken, *The Land Called Holy*, 191; Y. Salomon and M. Milner, *Jesus 2000*, 193; Murphy-O'Connor, *The Holy Land*, 34–35.

[297] Walker, *In the Steps of Jesus: An Illustrated Guide to the Places of the Holy Land*, 194.

[298] Left: Michael L. Russo. Photographed by Michael James Russo, April 28, 2012. Right: Todd Bolen/BiblePlaces.com, Holy Sepulchre Golgotha rock outcrop, tb010312335.

The Twelfth Station: Jesus Dies On The Cross

right of the altar, under a metal cover, one can see the crevice that was created in the rock when the cross was fixed into it. Salomon and Milner describe the fissure as reaching to the Chapel of Adam directly below.[299] Tradition has it that Christ died on the spot where Adam was buried.[300] As early as the third century, Origen was aware of a tradition that the body of Adam was buried where Christ was crucified.[301]

Figure 33. **Left:** The Chapel of Adam. This is a view of the lower part of the Rock of Calvary in the Chapel of Adam. This is the traditional burial site of Adam, based on the belief that Christ, the "New Adam," was crucified over Adam's grave. Directly in front of the altar is the section of Golgotha that shows the crack that was supposedly created during the earthquake after the crucifixion. **Right:** A closer view of the crack in Golgotha that is directly in front of the altar.[302]

---

[299] Salomon and Milner, *Jesus 2000*, 196; Murphy-O'Connor, *The Holy Land*, 52.

[300] Murphy-O'Connor, *The Holy Land*, 52.

[301] Wilken, *The Land Called Holy*, 94.

[302] Michael L. Russo. Photographed by Michael James Russo, April 23, 2012.

The Via Dolorosa

Figure 34. The altar at Calvary. Beneath the altar is a silver disk protecting the spot where Christ's cross was placed.[303]

For the six hours that Jesus hung on the cross, Matthew, Mark and Luke tell us that the earth was covered in darkness (Matt. 27:45; Mark 15:33; Luke 23:44). This is a reference to the Old Testament prophecies that describe the "Day of Judgment" as being marked by a sudden darkness (Joel 2:2). The scene after Jesus died was chaotic. The curtain of the Temple was torn in two, the earth shook, rocks were split, and tombs were opened. Many bodies of saints were raised and appeared to many. The old order had been overturned. Salvation and redemption were opened to all (cf. Matt. 27:51–53; Mark 15:38).

> If the birth of Jesus was marked by a sign in the heavens (a star's rising), His death is marked by signs on earth (a quake) and under the earth (tombs). His death brings judgment on the Temple but also the resurrection of the

---

[303] Michael L. Russo. Photographed by Michael James Russo, April 23, 2012.

The Twelfth Station: Jesus Dies On The Cross

saints of Israel. Human relationships to God have been changed and the cosmos has been transformed.[304]

Jesus conquered death, and in so doing secured the salvation of the world. Some may have viewed His death as an embarrassing end to a promising career. The Messiah crucified? Impossible! Those at the foot of the cross never doubted Jesus. They knew who He was, and the world would never be the same.

Figure 35. The altar inside the church is a rocky outcropping, which is the traditional place where the cross was placed. Archaeological excavations have demonstrated that this site was outside the city wall but close to one of its gates and thus would have been a good location for a crucifixion. Today this chapel is cared for by the Greek Orthodox Church.[305]

---

[304] Brown, *An Introduction to the New Testament*, 202.

[305] Michael L. Russo. Photographed by Michael James Russo, April 23, 2012.

CHAPTER 19

THE THIRTEENTH STATION: JESUS IS TAKEN DOWN FROM THE CROSS

After this, Joseph of Arimathea, secretly a disciple of Jesus for fear of the Jews, asked Pilate if he could remove the body of Jesus, and Pilate permitted it. So he came and took His body. (John 20:38)

Because it was a Friday, it was important to bury the body of Jesus before the Sabbath began at sunset. Scripture tells us that Joseph of Arimathea, a good and just man, went to Pilate to ask for the release of the body (cf. Matt. 27:57–58; cf. Luke 23:50–52; John 19:38). Joseph's name indicates that he originally came from the town of Ramathaim, north of Lydda.[306] However, according to these events, he must have been residing in the area. In the Syn-

---

[306] "Arimathea is usually identified with Ramathaim" (see 1 Sam 1:1). John R. Donahue and Daniel J. Harrington, *Sacra Pagina: The Gospel of Mark* (Collegeville, MN: The Liturgical Press, 2002), 453. In Hebrew, the town of Arimathea is known as Ramathaim. See Alban Butler and John Cumming, *Butler's Lives of the Saints* (Collegeville,

The Thirteenth Station: Jesus Is Taken Down From The Cross

optic Gospels, it appears that Joseph acted alone, but in John's Gospel, Joseph is joined by Nicodemus.[307] Nicodemus had not openly admitted that he believed in Jesus. Together, however, both men publicly gave Jesus an honorable burial.[308]

Pierre Barbet concludes that the body of Jesus was handled very gently. The nails were removed from his feet and the *patibulum* was lifted off the *stipes*.[309] He suggests that there were five people handling the body due to the combined weight of the body and the *patibulum*. Three men would be needed to lift the *patibulum* and the remaining two would have supported the trunk of Christ's body by means of a sheet. The sheet would have been twisted to make a band and placed across and under the chest. The body was then placed on a cloth on what is today called the stone of anointing, and the hands were detached from the *patibulum*.[310] Jesus's body was wrapped in a linen cloth along with perfumed spices (cf. Matt. 27:59–60; Mark 15:46; Luke 23:53; cf. John 19:40–41).

Station XIII is located between Station XI and Station XII in the Church of the Holy Sepulchre. This Station marks where Jesus was taken down from the cross and laid in His

---

MN: The Liturgical Press, 1998), 327; Daniel J. Harrington, "The Gospel According to Mark," in *NJBC*, §41-103, 628.

[307] R. Brown and others, "The Life of Jesus of Nazareth," in *BTBA*, 2007, 446.

[308] Brown, *An Introduction to the New Testament*, 358.

[309] Barbet's conclusion that the body of Jesus was handled with respect and gentleness is detailed in chapter 7 of his book *A Doctor at Calvary*. That particular chapter was written specifically for the doctors of the *Société de Saint Luc* (Bulletin of March, 1938). See Barbet, *A Doctor at Calvary*, 128. Barbet insists there was only one nail holding Jesus's feet. See Barbet, *A Doctor at Calvary*, 112.

[310] Barbet, *A Doctor at Calvary*, 130–132. Barbet uses the word "shroud," but I am using the word "cloth" to eliminate confusion with any reference to the Shroud of Turin.

mother's arms. The altar that marks Station XIII is named the Altar of Our Lady of Sorrows (Mater Dolorosa) and is dedicated to Mary. At the altar piece is a sixteenth-century gold-plated statue of the Madonna decorated with precious stones and a gold crown. The statue was given to the Church in 1788 by Queen Maria I Braganza of Portugal. It is housed in a glass cabinet. Pilgrims have subsequently hung gold gifts around the cabinet as offerings.[311]

Figure 36. The Altar of Our Lady of Sorrows (Mater Dolorosa).[312]

---

[311] Salomon, Milner, *Jesus 2000*, 196; Raymond Cohen, *Saving the Holy Sepulchre*, 82.

[312] Michael L. Russo. Photographed by Michael James Russo, April 23, 2012.

CHAPTER 20

THE TOMB IN A GARDEN

Now in the place where He had been crucified there was a garden, and in the garden a new tomb, in which no one had yet been buried. So they laid Jesus there because of the Jewish preparation day; for the tomb was close by. (John 19:41–42)

ecause Jesus's death took place on a Friday, His followers would have had to remove His body before the beginning of the Sabbath at sunset. Criminals were usually interred in a common grave without ceremony. Only someone with sufficient social or political standing could ask Pilate for the body of Jesus.[313] Joseph of Arimathea was one such man. He was a member of the Sanhedrin, and he went to Pilate to ask for the body of Jesus. Pilate was surprised that Jesus had died so quickly but granted Joseph's request. Joseph owned one of the rock-hewn tombs that were cut into the walls of the quarry that surrounded Golgotha. The tomb was new (John 19:41), and according to B. Pixner, it could only hold one

---

[313] R. Brown and others, "The Life of Jesus of Nazareth," in *BTBA*, 446.

body.[314] Pixner's comment, however, does create some confusion. Because Joseph of Arimathea was a wealthy man, he could have afforded a private tomb or he might have reserved his private resting place within the family tomb. Family tombs were common in the first century CE. Because Scripture only refers to "a tomb," (Matt. 27:60; Mark 15:46; Luke 23:53; John 19:41), it is difficult to determine whether the tomb might have been for more than one person.

Figure 37. The Tomb of the Kings. The two most common types of tombs in the first century CE are both found in this tomb complex. Loculi (kokhim) were long narrow shafts in which the deceased were placed and closed with a stone slab, which probably had the name of the occupant inscribed on it. Channels in the center of the shafts were probably carved to drain the water that seeped through the rock.[315]

---

[314] Pixner, *With Jesus in Jerusalem*, 148.

[315] Todd Bolen/BiblePlaces.com, Arcosolium in Tomb of Kings, tb042200201.

The Tomb In A Garden

Figure 38. Example of an *arcosolium* (arched tomb).[316]

The style of the tomb is critical information for identifying the actual location of the tomb because there is ongoing debate as to whether it is located in the Garden Tomb, recognized by many Protestants, or in the tomb located in the Church of the Holy Sepulchre, recognized by Catholic and Orthodox Christians. The Garden Tomb was not suggested as the tomb of Jesus until the nineteenth century, having only been discovered in 1867. At that time, it was just one among the many burial caves in and around Jerusalem. During his short stay in Jerusalem, between 1883 and 1884, Charles George Gordon, also known as General "Chinese" Gordon (a nickname he received for suppressing the 1864 Taiping Rebellion in China), identified Golgotha with a "scarp" located near a burial cave that was to become known as the "Garden Tomb" and which he argued was the burial place

---

[316] Todd Bolen/BiblePlaces.com, Hinnom Valley Second Temple period tomb arcosolium and loculi, tb110804043.

of Jesus. Gordon imagined the topography of Jerusalem in the shape of an entire skeleton. In his mind, he viewed the Temple Mount as the pelvis, and Solomon's quarries as the ribs. He identified the hill to the north of the Damascus Gate as "Golgotha" or "The Place of the skull" as mentioned in Scripture. It is still known today as "Gordon's Calvary."[317]

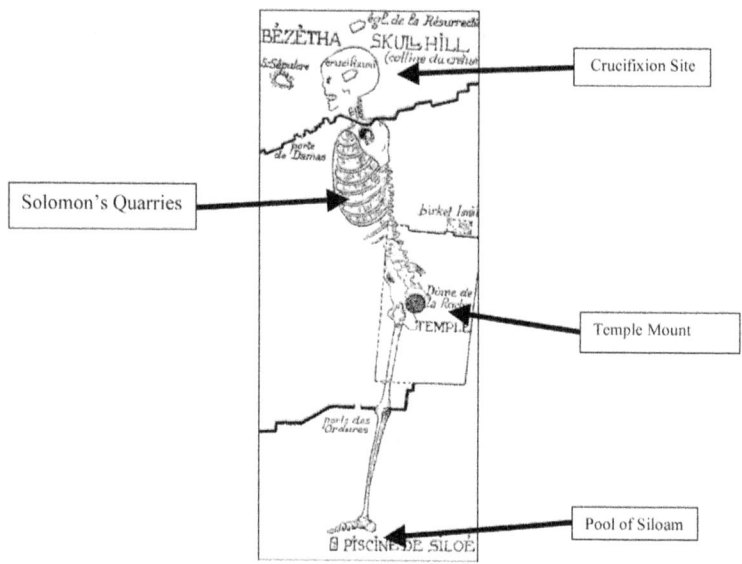

Figure 39. Gordon imagined the topography of Jerusalem as a skeleton. The skull is where he identified Golgotha. The Temple Mount marks the pelvis. The feet rest at the Pool of Siloam.[318]

Supporters of the Garden Tomb argue that it is outside the Old City walls; burials were not permitted inside the city at the time of Christ's crucifixion. The tomb was acquired

---

[317] Daniel Jacobs, *The Rough Guide to Israel and the Palestinian Territories* (New York: Rough Guides Publications, 1998), 354.

[318] Shanks, *The Jerusalem of Jesus*, 197. See also, Gabriel Barkay, "The Garden Tomb: Was Christ Buried Here?" *BAR*, (March/April, 1986), 43.

The Tomb In A Garden

by an influential group of Englishmen that included the Archbishop of Canterbury and went by the name the Garden Tomb Association. The adjacent area was landscaped to fit the description in the Gospel of John.[319] The site is maintained by the Anglican Church.[320]

There is ongoing debate concerning the location of Christ's tomb. There are those who recognize the Garden Tomb with its peaceful setting as the authentic tomb of Christ and those who accept the tomb located in the bustling and sometimes chaotic Church of the Holy Sepulchre. The "bustling" church, as it is referred to by P. Walker, does reflect a number of buildings and is the most likely candidate for containing the actual tomb of Christ.[321] According to J. Murphy-O'Connor, similar first century CE tombs were found in the area, and although archeological information is meager, the site in the church is compatible with the topographical information found in the Gospels (John 19:17, 41–2).[322] Recent stratigraphic excavations have corroborated the work of Constantine's archaeologists. Walls were discovered from a monumental structure that date back to the time of Hadrian. It is believed that this structure was the Temple of Aphrodite

---

[319] Ibid., 197.

[320] Salomon and Milner, *Jesus 2000*, 197.

[321] Walker, *In the Steps of Jesus*, 192, 193. J. Murphy-O'Connor comments, "One hopes for peace, but the ear is assailed by a cacophony of warring chants." Murphy-O'Connor, *The Holy Land*, 45. Webster T. Patterson states, "The pilgrim or visitor is often confronted by what appears to be a religious mob scene, complete with a cacophony of chants, processions, and liturgies." *Sacred Sites*, 48.

[322] Murphy-O'Connor, *The Holy Land*, 45, 141. Murphy-O'Connor asserts the configuration of the Garden Tomb is typical for a ninth-century BCE–seventh-century BCE tomb because the tombs of that period contained body benches extending from the wall. In the time of Christ, the burial chamber would have been in a straight line behind a vestibule. Each body bench (*arcosolium*) would have been set within an arch.

The Via Dolorosa

constructed over Christ's tomb. Tombs dating back to the first century CE and earlier have been discovered under the Church of the Holy Sepulchre, and the church is close to the place where Jesus was crucified.[323]

Archaeologists discovered that the Anglican Garden Tomb, which was discovered in the nineteenth century, was not used for burials at the time of Christ's crucifixion.[324] Prior to the crucifixion of Jesus, the area was used as a rock quarry.[325] When excavated, the only artifacts found in the tomb dated to the eighth or seventh century BCE. No coins or pottery were found to support the use of the tomb during the time of Christ's crucifixion. "Because it was reused in the Byzantine and Crusader periods, it could have been reused in the first century CE." However, there is no archaeological proof to support this claim.[326]

---

[323] Crossan and Reed, *Excavating Jesus*, 249.

[324] Shanks, *Jerusalem's Temple Mount*, 40. Both P. Walker and J. Murphy-O'Connor state there is evidence that the tomb located in the Church of the Holy Sepulchre is the actual tomb of Christ. See Walker, *In the Steps of Jesus*, 190; Murphy-O'Connor, *The Holy Land*, 45. Walker refers to the tomb in the Church of the Holy Sepulchre as the "traditional tomb of Jesus," (p. 195).

[325] Crossan and Reed, *Excavating Jesus*, 249. See Dan Bahat, "Does the Holy Sepulchre Church Mark the Burial of Jesus?" *Biblical Archaeology Review*. http:// www.bib-arch.org/online-exclusives/easter-06.asp.

[326] John J. Rousseau and Rami Arav, *Jesus and His World* (Minneapolis, MN: Augsburg Fortress, 1995), 104–109.

The Tomb In A Garden

Figure 40. The Garden Tomb. The adjacent area of the garden tomb was landscaped to match the description in John's Gospel. It is believed this tomb was not used for burials during the time of Christ. In 1974, it was discovered that this tomb was hewn during the First Temple Period.[327]

The original church complex of the Holy Sepulchre Basilica built by Constantine in the fourth century is on the site where his mother, Helena, supposedly found the cross on which Christ was crucified. Constantine built a rotunda over the tomb. Although the tomb was inside the city walls by the fourth century, in the twentieth century, archaeologists discovered that at Jesus's time, this tomb was, in fact, outside the city walls. This finding adds credence to belief that the tomb in the Church of the Holy Sepulchre is the actual tomb of Christ. If the tomb in the Church of the Holy Sepulchre was, in fact, inside the city walls at the time of Christ, it could not have been considered to be the actual tomb because burials took place outside the city walls.

---

[327] Todd Bolen/BiblePlaces.com, Garden Tomb, tb051703206.

The Via Dolorosa

Further evidence that the Church of the Holy Sepulchre marks Jesus's actual tomb comes from the writings of Eusebius. In the fourth century, Eusebius wrote that Hadrian built a temple to Venus/Aphrodite on the site where Constantine later built the Church of the Holy Sepulchre. Eusebius tells us that Hadrian wanted to obliterate an early memorial over the tomb of Jesus and went to great pains to cover it up.[328] When Constantine's mother, Helena, arrived in Jerusalem, she located the site of the crucifixion and resurrection under the temple of Venus. The cave containing Christ's tomb was discovered only after the temple and landfill were cleared from the site. The discovery exceeded all expectations. Constantine ordered that a "place of worship worthy of God" be built to testify to the resurrection. The burial cave was then cut away from the surrounding rock and enclosed in an *Aedicule* (little house). A rotunda known as the *Anastasis* was built over the *Aedicule*. In 638 CE, Muslim armies captured Jerusalem, and in 1009 CE, Constantine's church was destroyed and the burial cave was razed.[329] Fatimid Caliph Hakim's destruction of the church was so complete in 1009 CE that very little of original structure was left above ground.[330]

---

[328] Shanks, *Jerusalem's Temple Mount*, 41, 43. Archaeologists discovered tombs from the time of Christ under the Church of the Holy Sepulchre, noting that the Church stands on the site of a first-century burial ground. Hadrian built his new city, Aelia Capitolina, in 135 CE and built a temple to Aphrodite over the site of Christ's tomb. He "plowed up the Temple Mount." In doing so, he was conducting a traditional Roman ceremony, "founding a new city." Hadrian wanted to destroy all memories of the defeated people. See Yohanan Aharoni and Shmuel Ahituv, *The Jewish People* (New York, NY: The Continuum International Publishing Group, 2006), 99–100.

[329] Cohen, *Saving the Holy Sepulchre*, 3.

[330] Ibid., 202.

The Tomb In A Garden

Hoping to discover additional information concerning the validity of the claim being made for the Garden Tomb, in 1974, Israeli archaeologist Gabriel Barkay decided to study the material gathered since the 1880s about the First Temple and Second Temple Period tombs. He discovered that the Garden Tomb had the style and characteristics of a First Temple Period tomb. He determined that these findings disqualified the Garden Tomb because John's Gospel clearly states that Christ was buried in a new tomb: "Now in the place where He had been crucified was a garden, and in the garden a new tomb, in which no one had yet been buried. (John 19:41)." Barkay located some pottery believed to have been found in the Garden Tomb. The pottery dated back to the eighth or seventh century BCE. He then argued that the Garden Tomb was, in fact, hewn around that time. Barkay insists the tomb was originally in the center of cemetery dating back to the First Temple Period. He claims that there were no Second Temple Period tombs found in the area and that this particular tomb lies just south of the École Biblique.[331]

Many excavations have been made at the traditional sites of the New Testament events. However, the discoveries made at these sites usually date back only to the remains of churches and shrines from the fourth century.

---

[331] Shanks, *Jerusalem: An Archaeological Biography*, 200. Dan Cole, Professor of Religion at Lake Forest College, Lake Forest, Illinois, states that the Garden Tomb dates to an Iron Age tomb (8–6 century BCE) and was later adapted for use. See *BAS, Biblical World in Pictures*, NT99. The Garden Tomb remains an important shrine for many Christians. Jerome Murphy-O'Connor states that the configuration of the Garden Tomb is typical of tombs found in the 9–7 century BCE, *The Holy Land*, 141.

CHAPTER 21

THE *AEDICULE*

When the Church of the Holy Sepulchre was first built in the Byzantine period, it was one of two separate structures constructed by Constantine on the site identified by Helena. One site consisted of a rotunda with a dome that marked the tomb of Christ. The other site was a basilica church. The rotunda and the basilica were separated by a courtyard that was enclosed in a colonnaded portico.[332] "The burial cave faced the rising sun and had been cut away from the surrounding rock. It was enclosed in an *Aedicule*, a 'little house.'"[333] The *Aedicule* was a shrine constructed over the tomb that was supported by columns.[334] When the Church of the Holy Sepulchre was originally built, the tomb was separated from the rock, and the magnificent rotunda (*Anastasis*) was built around it. Today, the small *Aedicule*

---

[332] Shanks, *Jerusalem's Temple Mount*, 10; Murphy-O'Connor identifies four elements: an atrium, the basilica, an open courtyard, and the tomb in a circular edifice. The construction of the church began in 326 CE. It was dedicated in 335 CE. *The Holy Land*, 47.

[333] Cohen, *Saving the Holy Sepulchre*, 3.

[334] Shanks, *Jerusalem's Temple Mount*, 40.

The Aedicule

incorporates all that is left of the cave that was revered as Jesus's empty tomb. The edifice was renovated in the Crusader period (1095–1291 CE), and the tomb was completely overlaid with marble. The tomb was then damaged during a fire in 1808, and the dome of the rotunda collapsed.[335] The present neo-Byzantine *Aedicule* was built in 1810.[336]

Constantine is credited with having his architects remove the bedrock from the hillside to create the *Anastasis* (rotunda) that is directly over the *Aedicule*. The vestibule of the *Aedicule* is called the Chapel of the Angel. Traditionally, this marks the place where the angel appeared on Easter morning. The original bedrock survived the attack by Fatimid Caliph Hakim in 1009 CE and is still preserved in the wall that separates the vestibule from the inner burial chamber and also beneath the burial shelf.[337]

---

[335] Salomon and Milner, *Jesus 2000*, 197; Murphy-O'Connor, *The Holy Land*, 52.

[336] Cohen, *Saving the Holy Sepulchre*, 3.

[337] BAS, *Biblical World in Pictures*, photo JA106.

Figure 41: The *Aedicule*. This structure preserves the location of Christ's tomb. Historically, this has been the revered location of the tomb.[338]

---

[338] Michael L. Russo. Photographed by Michael James Russo, April 23, 2012.

CHAPTER 22

THE TOMB OF CHRIST

> *After he had taken the body down, he wrapped it in a linen cloth and laid Him in a rock-hewn tomb in which no one had been buried. It was the day of preparation, and the Sabbath was about to begin. The women who had come from Galilee followed behind, and when they had seen the tomb and the way in which His body was laid in it, they returned and prepared spices and perfumed oils.*
> (Luke 24:53–56)

Eusebius tells us that in an effort to locate the tomb of Christ, Constantine ordered the destruction of the forum and the pagan temples that were built in that area during the second century CE. One of the few known archaeological digs of ancient history had been gloriously successful.[339] Eusebius gives a detailed account of the discovery in *The Life of Constantine*:

---

[339] Walker, *In the Steps of Jesus*, 188.

Constantine decided that he ought to make universally famous and revered the most blessed site in Jerusalem of the Saviour's [sic] resurrection. . . . This very cave of the Saviour some godless and wicked people had planned to make invisible to mankind. . . . They brought earth from somewhere outside and covered up the whole place . . . and so hid the cave beneath a great quantity of soil. Then . . . they built a gloomy sanctuary to the impure demon of Aphrodite. . . . [Constantine] did not negligently allow that place to remain smothered by all sorts of filthy rubbish. . . . At a word of command those contrivances of fraud were demolished from top to bottom, and the houses of error were dismantled and destroyed.

The Emperor gave further orders that all rubble of stones and timbers from the demolitions should be taken and dumped a long way from the site . . . [and] that the site should be excavated to a great depth. . . . As stage by stage the underground site was exposed, at last against all expectation the revered and all-hallowed Testimony (Martyrion) of the Saviour's Resurrection was itself revealed, and the cave, the holy of holies, took on the appearance of a representation of the Saviour's return to life. Thus after its descent into darkness it came forth again to the light, and it enabled those who came as visitors to see plainly the story of the wonders wrought there, testifying by acts louder than any voice to the resurrection of the Saviour.[340]

Eusebius repeatedly refers to the place as a cave. In the Mediterranean world, caves were sacred places whose darkness and inaccessibility made them particularly suitable places to encounter the divine. Eusebius calls the cave where Christ was buried the "sacred cave" or the "most holy cave." He also tells us that the cave had been covered with "impurities." The entire area had to be cleansed because it

---

[340] Ibid., 188. Walker is quoting from Eusebius's *The Life of Constantine*, 3:25–28.

had been "stained." The workers were instructed to dig deep and take the remnants of the demolished houses as well as the stones and soil a far distance from the site. In *The Life of Constantine*, Eusebius stated that the site was holy even before the burial and the resurrection of Jesus. "He used the phrase, 'from the beginning' suggesting that he integrated the historical event of the Resurrection to an older cosmogonic myth."[341]

Bargil Pixner, OSB, provides a touching picture of Jesus's burial. Jesus was taken down from the cross, and His body was anointed and wrapped in linen shrouds. The small funeral procession consisting of Joseph of Arimathea, Nicodemus, and the women who remained through the entire Passion made their way through the garden to the tomb. While the women watched and sobbed, Jesus's body was carried down a few stone steps, through a low square-shaped opening in the rock, into an anteroom, and finally placed in the inner room on the bench of an *arcosolium* (arched tomb). They wrapped a burial cloth around His head and left the tomb. They rolled a large round stone in front of the entrance to the tomb, fastened it with wedges, and went home.[342]

Archeologists have made several probes into the various claims concerning the accuracy of the locations of sites claiming to be Christ's tomb. As a result, Gordon's Calvary, the Garden Tomb, and all other sites except the tomb in the Church of the Holy Sepulchre have been discounted by virtually all scientific scholarship.[343] The tomb located in the Church of the

---

[341] Wilken, *The Land Called Holy*, 89. J. Smith also references this comment made by Eusebius in *Viti Constantini* 3.28, 30. See Jonathan Z. Smith, *To Take Place* (Chicago, IL: University of Chicago Press, 1987), 83.

[342] Pixner, *With Jesus in Jerusalem*, 148. Pixner uses the word "shroud" rather than the term "linen cloth."

[343] Rousseau and Arav, *Jesus and His World*, 109. J. Murphy-O'Connor agrees that the Garden Tomb is not the place where Christ was

Holy Sepulchre is regarded as the actual tomb of Jesus. It is the older location, and it is supported by traditions that date back to at least the fourth century.[344] The structure that today surrounds the tomb was built by the Greek Orthodox after a fire that occurred in the nineteenth century. It is divided into two parts. There is an anteroom that is named the Chapel of the Angel, and there is the Chapel of the Holy Tomb.

Figure 42. **Left:** Constantine's magnificent rotunda directly over the *Aedicule* of the tomb of Christ. The structure seen in the center of the photo is the *Aedicule* that protects the holiest site in Christianity. **Right:** The holiest site in Christianity. This slab is believed to be where Christ's body was laid in the tomb.[345]

---

buried. "Garden Tomb, Jerusalem," at Sacred Destinations. http://www.sacred-destinations.com/israel/jerusalem-garden-tomb.htm.

[344] Crossan and Reed, *Excavating Jesus*, 248.

[345] Michael L. Russo. Photographed by Michael James Russo, April 23, 2012.

The empty tomb is located on the right of the inner chamber and is covered by a cracked marble slab. The chamber is very small and can only fit a few people at a time.[346] Many visitors are frustrated with the confined space and the size of the line of pilgrims waiting to get into the tomb. It is good to remember that this is not simply a museum. It is a place that is alive with the sounds of worship and song that are rooted in faith expressed with devotion.[347]

Figure 43. The Chapel of the Angel and entrance to Christ's tomb.[348]

---

[346] Salomon and Milner, *Jesus 2000*, 197.
[347] Cohen, *Saving the Holy Sepulchre*, 4.
[348] Michael L. Russo. Photographed by Michael James Russo, April 23, 2012.

CHAPTER 23

THE FOURTEENTH STATION: JESUS IS LAID IN THE TOMB

If a man guilty of a capital offense is put to death and his corpse hung on a tree, it shall not remain on the tree overnight. You shall bury it the same day. (Deut. 22:22–23)

Taking the body, Joseph wrapped it [in] clean linen and laid it in his new tomb that he had hewn in the rock. Then he rolled a huge stone across the entrance to the tomb and departed. (Matt. 27:59–60)

Proper burial for the dead was an important issue for the Jews. The law in Deuteronomy was clear. The dead body must be buried on the same day (Deut. 21:23). No corpse must be left unburied overnight. The reasons for this were both for sanitation and to avoid defilement of the body. The Jews knew the law and were strict about adhering to it. The Gospel of Mark tells us that Mary Magdalene and Mary, the mother of Joses, saw where Jesus was laid (Mark 15:47. See also Matt. 27:61; Luke 23:55). They would return with spices and ointment to properly anoint the body.

The Fourteenth Station: Jesus Is Laid In The Tomb

It was customary for family to visit the grave for three days after the death. In Jesus's case, a stone was placed in front of the tomb to ensure that the disciples would not steal the body and proclaim that Jesus rose from the dead.[349] Because there was little time to bury Jesus before the Sabbath, the Jewish traditions of washing and anointing the body had to be delayed. However, John tells us that Joseph of Arimathea and Nicodemus prepared the body as was customary (cf. John 19:39–40). Mark and Luke both tell us that the women returned on the first day of the week with spices to anoint Jesus (cf. Mark 16:1-2; Luke 24:1). Matthew and John state that the women went to the tomb but do not mention anything about spices or anointing (Matt. 28:1; John 20:1). The fact that the women returned with spices does suggest that the burial had been incomplete. In Jewish custom though, a second anointing was also an expression of respect. It is important to note that none of the Evangelists wrote that the women returned to the tomb to wash the body because it had not been properly prepared.[350]

Although there is no mention of John or Mary, the mother of Jesus, accompanying the body to the tomb, Jewish custom would have expected them to have been present. The Jews considered it extremely important for family, close friends, and relatives to accompany the body under normal circumstances. Even strangers who were present were expected to accompany the body as it was carried to

---

[349] Bennett, *Sacred Blood*, 129–130. For a detailed explanation of Jewish burial customs, see Kaufman Kohler, "Burial," in *The Jewish Encyclopedia*, 2002 ed., 432–437. http://www.jewishencyclopedia.com/view_page.jsp?artid=1607&letter=B&pid=0.

[350] Bennett, *Sacred Blood*, 130. Judah David Eisenstein provides a detailed explanation of the Jewish ceremony of washing a body before burial. See Judah David Eisenstein, "Taharah," in *The Jewish Encyclopedia*, 668. http://www.jewishencyclopedia.com/view_page.jsp?artid=18&letter=T&pid=0.

the grave. Criminals who were executed by a Jewish court would have to be interred in a court's graveyard. This was a special cemetery provided for that purpose. According to the law, private individuals were not allowed to bury such persons, and no one was permitted to mourn them. Convicts who were executed by the order of the Roman governor had to be buried and mourned like anyone who died a natural death. Because Jesus was sentenced to death by a Roman court, He was entitled to the benefits of a traditional Jewish burial and mourning period. The traditional mourning ritual would require that those present at the foot of the cross also be present at the burial.[351] Scripture says nothing about the whereabouts of the apostles during the burial. However, the prophet Zechariah and the Gospel writers shed some light on their disappearance.

> Awake, O sword, against my shepherd, against the man who is my associate, says the Lord of Hosts. Strike the shepherd that the sheep may be dispersed. (Zech. 13:7)

> Then Jesus said to them, "This night you will have your faith in me shaken, for it is written: 'I will strike the shepherd, and the sheep of the flock will be dispersed.'" (Matt. 26:31; Mark 14:27)

> Behold, the hour is coming and has arrived when each of you will leave me alone. (John 16:32)

---

[351] Bennett, *Sacred Blood*, 131–132. Kaufman Kohler, "Burial," in *The Jewish Encyclopedia*, 2002 ed., 432–437. http://www.jewishencyclopedia.com/view_page.jsp?artid=1607&letter=B&pid=0.

The Fourteenth Station: Jesus Is Laid In The Tomb

The apostles disappeared just as Scripture foretold. In this act of abandonment, the prophecy of Zechariah was fulfilled, just as was the case in the Passion and death of Christ. "The Holy Sepulcher is a building dedicated to a single belief shared by all Christians, that humanity was saved through the sacrifice of Jesus Christ."[352] Eusebius uses the term *martyrion* (a place that bears witness) to designate the basilica that was constructed adjacent to the site of the tomb. He calls the tomb of Christ "a *martyrion* of the saving resurrection."[353]

According to W. Patterson, today the Church of Holy Sepulchre is basically the same structure that the Crusaders left behind after they conquered Jerusalem in 1099. There is little evidence of Constantine's fourth-century church due to its destruction by the Persians in 614. It was poorly restored and was destroyed again by Egyptian Caliph Hakim in 1009. With only the rotunda left, the Crusaders built the church into the form that it is today. It was almost destroyed by fire in 1808 and suffered severe damage in an earthquake that struck the area in 1927. Since the 1950s, the Greeks, Armenians, and Catholics have been attempting to restore the structure to some of its original beauty.[354] Constantine attempted to replace the original glory of the Temple when he planned the construction of the basilica that was to be in front of the tomb of Christ. Eusebius states that the basilica "faced the rising sun" and was magnificent in its beauty. Similar to the Jewish Temple, Constantine included cedars of Lebanon in the construction. Eusebius declared, "How true it is that the 'latter glory of this house exceeds the former.'"[355]

---

[352] Cohen, *Saving the Holy Sepulcher*, 4.

[353] Wilken, *The Land Called Holy*, 92.

[354] Patterson, *Sacred Sites*, 47–48, 50; Salomon and Milner, *Jesus 2000*, 196; Murphy-O'Connor, *The Holy Land*, 48–50.

[355] Shanks, *Jerusalem: An Archaeological Biography*, 206.

The Via Dolorosa

If visitors to the holy site expect to find a peaceful structure ideal for meditation, contemplation, and prayer, they will be sadly disappointed. It is very possible that the visitors would be confronted with what could be called a religious mob scene. This would be especially true on Fridays when processions of cross-carrying pilgrims fill the Via Dolorosa. It goes without saying that the Lenten and Easter seasons are the most crowded. Chants, processions, and liturgies involving Greek Orthodox, Armenians, Roman Catholics, and Copts abound.[356] Father Jerome Murphy-O'Connor describes the current atmosphere:

> One looks for numinous light, but it is dark and cramped. One hopes for peace, but the ear is assailed by a cacophony of warring chants. One desires holiness, only to encounter a jealous possessiveness; the six groups of occupants—Latin Catholics, Greek Orthodox, Armenians, Syrians, Copts, Ethiopians—watch one another suspiciously for any infringement of rights. The frailty of humanity is nowhere more apparent than here; it epitomizes the human condition. The empty who come to be filled leave desolate.[357]

As previously mentioned, the tomb is divided into two parts. There is an anteroom known as the Chapel of the Angel, and there is the Chapel of the Holy Tomb. In the Chapel of the Angel, there is a piece of stone that is believed to be part of the stone that was rolled away from Christ's

---

[356] Patterson, *Sacred Sites*, 48; Murphy-O'Connor, *The Holy Land*, 45; Walker, *In the Steps of Jesus*, 192.

[357] Shanks, *Jerusalem: An Archaeological Biography*, 210; Murphy-O'Connor, *The Holy Land*, 45.

tomb on Easter morning.³⁵⁸ The empty tomb is covered with a simple cracked marble slab. Only three or four people can enter the tomb at any one time.³⁵⁹

Figure 44. **Left:** The Chapel of the Angel showing what is believed to be a piece of the stone that was rolled away from Christ's tomb.³⁶⁰

John tells us that Jesus knew His hour had come to pass from this world to the Father and that He knew everything that was going to happen (John 13:1, 18:4). This word "knowing" that John uses indicates that Jesus went to His

---

³⁵⁸ John Spier, Sacred Destinations.com, "Photo Gallery: The Church of the Holy Sepulcher." http://www.sacred-destinations.com/israel/jerusalem-holy-sepulchre-pictures /slides/edicule-room1-cc-john-spier.htm.

³⁵⁹ Salomon, Milner, *Jesus 2000*, 197.

³⁶⁰ Michael L. Russo. Photographed by Michael James Russo, April 23, 2012.

death in the full awareness of the salvific significance of what was happening.[361]

Cyril of Jerusalem wrote, "God has opened his arms on the Cross in order to span the limits of the earth's orb."[362] This is the gift of Christ's sacrifice, the gift of God's love. From all eternity, God has thought of us lovingly. G. Emmett Carter states, "He brought us to the life of earth and the life of grace. He surrounded us with His angels and His loving providence. God became man out of love for us and He died on the Cross in the excess of His love."[363]

"So God in His suffering spread out His arms and gathered in the circle of the earth, so as to announce that, from the rising of the sun to its setting, a future people would be gathered under His wings."[364] At the core of our faith is the true understanding of the cross. In sending His Son to suffer and die for our sins, God demonstrated His unlimited love for all people. When we view the cross as God's great sign of love, we gain a clearer understanding of Jesus's statement, "Pick up your cross and follow me" (Matt. 16:24). Just as Jesus poured out His love on the cross for us, we are called to treat others with unconditional love—the type of love that involves personal sacrifice.[365] We are called upon to let God use our eyes to see those around us who are hurting, our ears to listen to their concerns, our hands to reach out to them in compassion, and our hearts to spread the unending love that God has to give.

---

[361] De La Potterie, *The Hour of Jesus*, 140.

[362] Von Balthasar, *Mysterium Paschale*, 129–130.

[363] Very Rev. Canon G. Emmett Carter, *Psychology and the Cross* (Milwaukee, WI: Bruce Publishing Company, 1959), 67.

[364] Von Balthasar, *Mysterium Paschale*, 130.

[365] Thomas Zanzig, *Jesus the Christ* (Winona, MN: Saint Mary's Press, 2000), 184.

CONCLUSION

The goal of this work was to provide a deeper understanding of the Passion and death of our Lord Jesus Christ so that we can grow in the knowledge of God's love for us. The Via Dolorosa is a permanent gift to us. It is a constant reminder of what Jesus suffered, where He suffered, and how He suffered so that humanity could be reconciled to the Father. Meditating on the Stations of the Cross is not just reserved for the Lenten season in preparation for Easter. The Passion and death of Jesus Christ should be in our minds and in our hearts daily, for it is in understanding that great love that we can gain strength and draw ourselves closer to God.

St. Jerome tells us, "When we pray we speak to God but when we read, God speaks to us."[366] We need to use all that is at our disposal to learn about and communicate the salvific work of Jesus. It is with that thought in mind that the goals for this work were established: to provide a tool for prayer, reflection, meditation, contemplation, education, and reconciliation.

---

[366] This statement was included in Father Ronald Tangen's "Preface to 1983 Holy Year Edition," in Liguori, *The Passion and Death of Jesus Christ*.

So we are ambassadors for Christ, as if God were appealing through us. We implore you on behalf of Christ, be reconciled to God. (2 Cor. 20)

WORKS CITED

Aharoni, Yohanan, and Shmuel Ahituv, *The Jewish People.* New York, NY: The Continuum International Publishing Group, 2006.

Anderson, Bernard, W. *Out of the Depths: The Psalms Speak to Us Today.* Louisville, KY: John Knox Press, 2000.

Anderson, Leith. *Jesus: An Intimate Portrait of the Man, His, Land, and His People.* Minneapolis, MN: Bethany House, 2005.

Auld, Alan Graeme, and Margreet Laura Steiner. *Jerusalem I: From the Bronze Age to the Maccabees.* Macon, GA: Mercer University Press, 1996.

Barbet, Pierre, MD. *A Doctor at Calvary.* Fort Collins, CO: Roman Catholic Books, 1953.

Barkay, Gabriel. "The Garden Tomb: Was Christ Buried Here?" *Biblical Archaeology Review* (March/April 1986): 43.

Beitzel, Barry J. *Biblica: The Bible Atlas.* Hauppauge, NY: Barron's Educational Series, Inc., 2007.

Benedict XVI. *Spiritual Thoughts.* Canada: USCCB Publishing, 2007.

Bennett, Janice. *Sacred Blood, Sacred Image.* Little, CO: Libri de Hispania, 2001.

Bialas, Martin, CP. *The Mysticism of the Passion in St. Paul of the Cross*. San Francisco, CA: Ignatius Press, 1990.

Blinzler, J. *The Trial of Jesus*. Westminster, MD: Newman 1959.

Boas, Adrian, J. *Jerusalem in the Time of the Crusades*. New York, NY: Routledge, 2001.

Bond, Helen K. *Pontius Pilate in History and Interpretation*. New York, NY: Cambridge University Press, 1998.

Brown, Raymond E., SS. *A Crucified Christ in Holy Week*. Collegeville, MN: The Liturgical Press, 1986.

———. *An Introduction to the New Testament*. New York, NY: Doubleday, 1997.

Brown, Raymond, E., SS, Joseph A. Fitzmyer, SJ, and Roland, E. Murphy, O.Carm. *The New Jerome Biblical Commentary*. Upper Saddle River, NJ: Prentice Hall, 1990.

Buby, Bertrand, SM. *Mary of Galilee, Volume 1*. Staten Island, NY: Alba House, 1994.

Butler, Alban, and John Cumming. *Butler's Lives of the Saints*. Collegeville, MN: The Liturgical Press, 1998.

Carter, Warren. *Pontius Pilate, Portraits of a Roman Governor*. Collegeville, MN: Liturgical Press, 2003.

Casey, Michael. *Sacred Reading: The Art of Lectio Divina*. Liguori, MO: Liguori/Triumph, 1996.

Casson, Lionel. *Travel in the Ancient World*. Baltimore, MD: Johns Hopkins University Press, 1994.

Champlin, Joseph M. *The Stations of the Cross with Pope John Paul II*. Liguori, MO: Liguori Publications, 1994.

Cohen, Raymond. *Saving the Holy Sepulchre: How Rival Christians Came to Rescue Their Holiest Shrine*. New York, NY: Oxford University Press, 2008.

Coogan, Michael D. *The Old Testament*. New York, NY: Oxford University Press, 2006.

Works Cited

Crossan, John Dominic, and Jonathan Reed. *Excavating Jesus: Beneath the Stones, Behind the Texts.* New York: Harper Collins Publishers, 2001.

Crossan, John Dominic, and N. T. Wright. *The Resurrection of Jesus.* Minneapolis, MN: Fortress Press, 2005.

Crown-Tamir, Hela. *How to Walk in the Footsteps of Jesus and the Prophets.* Jerusalem: Gefejn Publishing House LTD, 2000.

De La Potterie, Ignace, SJ. *The Hour of Jesus: The Passion and the Resurrection of Jesus According to John.* Staten Island, NY: Alba House, 1997.

De Liguori, St. Alphonsus. *The Passion and the Death of Jesus Christ.* Brooklyn, NY, The Redemptorist Fathers, 1927.

Deluxe Then and Now Bible Maps. Torrance, CA: Rose Publishing Company, 2007.

Donahue, John R., and Daniel J. Harrington. *Sacra Pagina: The Gospel of Mark.* Collegeville, MN: The Liturgical Press, 2002.

Elliott, Walter. *The Life of Jesus Christ: Embracing the Entire Gospel.* New York: The Catholic Book Exchange, 1908.

Emmett Carter, Canon G, Very Rev. *Psychology and the Cross.* Milwaukee, WI: Bruce Publishing Company, 1959.

Fitzmeyer, Joseph A. *To Advance the Gospel: New Testament Studies.* Grand Rapids, MI: Eerdmans Publishing Company, 1998.

Gonen, Rivka. *Biblical Holy Places: An Illustrated Guide.* Mahwah, NJ: Paulist Press, 2000.

The Gospel of Nicodemus Formerly Called the Acts of Pontius Pilate. Whitefish, MT: Kessinger Publishing, 2004.

Grabbe, Lester L. "Ethnic Groups in Jerusalem." In *Jerusalem in Ancient History and Tradition,* ed. Thomas

L. Thompson, 145–146. New York: Continuum International Publishing Group, 2004.

Habermas, Gary R. *The Risen Jesus and Future Hope.* Lanham, MD: Rowman & Littlefield Publishers, Inc., 2003.

———. *The Historical Jesus.* Joplin, MO: College Press Publishing Company, 1996.

Hall, Thelma. *Too Deep for Words: Rediscovering Lectio Divina.* Mahwah, NJ: Paulist Press, 1988.

Hall, Thomas N. "The Euangelium Nichodemi and Vindicta Saluatoris in Anglo-Saxon England," in *Two Old English Apocrypha and Their Manuscript Source*, ed. J.E. Cross, 72–74. Cambridge: Cambridge University Press, 1996.

Hand, John Oliver, and Petrus Christus. "Some Thoughts on the Iconography of the Head of Christ." *Metropolitan Museum Journal*, vol. 27, 1992.

Hengel, Martin. *Crucifixion.* Philadelphia, PA: Fortress Press, 1977.

Hobart, William Kirk, Rev. *The Medical Language of St. Luke: A Proof from Internal Evidence That 'The Gospel According to St. Luke," and "The Acts of the Apostles," Were Written by the Same Person and That the Writer Was a Medical Man."* Dublin: Hodges, Figgis and Company, 1882.

Hoehner, Harold W. *Chronological Aspects of the Life of Christ.* Grand Rapids, MI: Zondervan, 1978.

Holloway, Richard. *A Death in Jerusalem.* London: Faith Press, 1986.

Houselander, Caryll. *The Way of the Cross.* Liguori, MO: Liguori Publications, 2002.

Jacobs, Daniel. *The Rough Guide to Israel and the Palestinian Territories.* New York: Rough Guides Publications, 1998.

Works Cited

Janecko, Benedict, OSB. *The Psalms: Heartbeat of Life and Worship*. St. Meinrad, IN: St. Meinrad Archabbey, 1995.

Jenkins, Philip. *Hidden Gospels*. New York, NY: Oxford University Press, 2001.

Josephus. "The Life against Apion," "The Jewish War," and "Jewish Antiquities." *Josephus*. 9 vols. Translated by H. St. J. Thackeray, MA, Ralph Marcus, and Louis H. Feldman. Loeb Classical Library. Cambridge, MA: Harvard University Press, 1926–1963.

Kempis, Thomas Á. *On the Passion of Christ According to the Four Evangelists*. San Francisco, CA: Ignatius Press, 2004.

Kreeft, Peter, and Ronald K. Tacelli. *Handbook of Christian Apologetics*. Downers Grove, IL: InterVarsity Press, 1994.

Lake, Kirsopp. *Eusebius: The Ecclesiastical History, Volume I*. London, England: Harvard University Press, 1998.

Macpherson, Duncan. *Pilgrim Preacher: Palestine, Pilgrimage, and Preacher*. Trowbridge, England: Cromwell Press, 2004.

Maier, Paul L. *Pontius Pilate*. Grand Rapids, MI: Kregel Publications, 1968.

Martin, Regis. *Suffering of Love*. San Francisco, CA: Ignatius Press, 2006.

Murphy-O'Connor, Jerome, OP. *The Holy Land: An Oxford Archaeological Guide from Earliest Times to 1700*. New York: Oxford University Press, 1998.

Neuhaus, Richard John. *Death on a Friday Afternoon*. New York, NY: Basic Books, 2000.

Norman, H. *A Guide to the Christian Churches in the East*. Elkhart, IN: Mission Focus, 1989.

Notovich, Nocholas. *The Unknown Life of Jesus Christ*. New York, NY: R. F. Fenno and Company, 1890.

Packer, J. I., and M. C. Tenney, eds. *Illustrated Manners and Customs of the Bible*. Nashville, TN: Thomas Nelson Publishers, 1908.

Patterson, Webster T. *Sacred Sites*. Mahwah, NJ: Paulist Press, 2004.

Philo. "Embassy to Gaius." In *Philo*. 10 vols. vol 2. Translated by F. H. Colson. Loeb Classical Library. Cambridge, MA: Harvard University Press, 1962.

Pixner, Bargil, OSB. *With Jesus in Jerusalem: His First and Last Days in Judea*. Israel: Corazin Publishing, 1996.

Rhodes, James F. "The Pardoner's Vernycle and His Vera Icon." *Modern Language Studies*. vol. 13, no. 2, 1963.

Rooney, Gerard, CP. *The Mystery of Calvary*. New York, NY: Macmillan Company, 1959.

Rousseau, John J., and Rami Arav. *Jesus and His World*. Minneapolis, MN: Augsburg Fortress, 1995.

Ruffin, C. Bernard. *Padre Pio: The True Story*. Huntington, IN: Our Sunday Visitor Publishing Division, 1991.

Salomon, Y. *Jesus 2000*, ed. by D. Salomon. Israel: Alpha Communication Ltd., 1998.

Schneiders, Sandra M. *Written That You May Believe: Encountering Jesus in the Fourth Gospel*. New York, NY: The Crossroads Publishing Company, 2003.

Scudamore, Rev. William Edward, MA. *A Dictionary of Christian Antiquities, Volume 1*. Hartford, CT: The J.B. Burr Publishing Company, 1880.

Shanks, Hershel. *Jerusalem: An Archaeological Biography*. New York, NY: Random House, 1995.

———. *Jerusalem's Temple Mount: From Solomon to the Golden Dome*. New York, NY: Continuum International Publishing Group, Inc., 2007.

Smith, Jonathan Z. *To Take Place*. Chicago, IL: University of Chicago Press, 1987.

Works Cited

Stroud, William, MD. *The Physical Cause of the Death of Christ*. New York, NY: D. Appleton and Company, 1871.

Tajra, Harry W. *The Trial of St. Paul*. Tübingen, Germany: Mohr, 1989.

Von Balthasar, Hans Urs, *Mysterium Paschale*. San Francisco, CA: Ignatius Press, 2000.

Von Balthasar, Hans Urs, and Joseph Cardinal Ratzinger. *Mary: The Church at the Source*. San Francisco, CA: Ignatius Press, 2005.

Walker, Peter. *In the Steps of Jesus: An Illustrated Guide to the Places of the Holy Land*. Oxford, England: Lion Hudson Publishing, 2006.

The Way of the Cross. Baltimore, MD: Barton-Cotton, Inc., 1965.

Whiston, William. *The New Complete Works of Josephus*. Grand Rapids, MI: Kregel Publications, 1999.

Wilken, Robert L. *The Land Called Holy*. New Haven: Yale University Press, 1992.

Wilkinson, John. *Egeria's Travels*. Oxford: Oxbow Books, 1999.

— — —. *Jerusalem Pilgrims before the Crusades*. Warminster: England, 2002.

Wilson, Edward. *In Scripture Lands: New Views of Sacred Places*. London: The Religious Tract Society, 1891.

Zanzig, Thomas. *Jesus the Christ*. Winona, MN: Saint Mary's Press, 2000.

Zugibe, Frederick. *The Crucifixion of Jesus: A Forensic Study*. New York, NY: M. Evans and Company, 2005.

ELECTRONIC WORKS CITED

"Armenian, Greek Worshippers Come to Blows at Jesus' Tomb." *The Associated Press*. Available from www.haaretz.com/hasen/spages/976409.html.

Babylonian Talmud, Book 9: Tracts Maccoth, Shebuoth, Eduyoth, Abuda Zara, and Horiot. Translation by Michael L. Rodkinson, 1918. http://sacred-texts.com.

Bahat, Dan. "Does the Holy Sepulchre Church Mark the Burial of Jesus?" *Biblical Archaeology Review*. http://www.bib-arch.org/online-exclusives/easter-06.asp.

Biblical Archaeology Society. "Biblical World in Pictures." *Biblical Archaeology Review*, 2006, [CD-ROM] Washington, DC: Libronix Library System Software, 2006.

The Biblical World in Pictures; BAS Biblical World in Pictures CD, SNT52.

"Church of All Nations (Basilica of the Agony)." Sacred Destinations. Available from www.sacred-destinations.com/Israel/Jerusalem-church-of-all-nations.htm.

"Crucifixion." DVD. A&E Television Networks. New York, NY: New Video, 2008.

"The Crucifixion of Christ, A Return to the Cross." DVD. Directed by Mark E. Seremet. Ligonier, PA: Bema Publishing, 2004.

"Did Jesus Really Die on a Cross?" Jehovah's Witness Official Web Site. www.watchtower.org/e/200604a/article_01.htm.

Drugs.com, *Stedman's Medical Dictionary*, s.v. "Hematridosis." http://www.drugs.com/dict/hematidrosis.html.

Edwards, William D, MD, Wesley J Gabel, MDiv, and Floyd E. Hosmer, MS, AMI,. "The Physical Death of Jesus Christ." *The Journal of the American Medical Association*, vol. 255 number 11 (26 March 1986). http://www.bibleanswer.com/x_death.htm.

Goldberg, G. J. "The Roman Army: Key Concepts." London: Greenhill Books, 1998. http://www.members.aol.com/FlJosephus2/romanArmy.htm.

"How Jesus Died: The Final 18 Hours." DVD. Produced and Directed by John Dauer. Valencia CA: Trinity Pictures, 2004.

Makarios, Hieromonk. Feast of Saint Haralombos." *The Synaxarion: The Lives of the Saints of the Orthodox Church*. Chalkidike, Greece: Holy Convent of the Annunciation of Our Lady, 2001. http://www.goarch.org/en/special/listen_learn_share/haralambos/learn/index.asp..

My Holy Land. Available from www.my-holyland.com/site.php?site_id=42&category_id=1.

"Once Again Monks Come to Blows at Church of Holy Sepulcher." *The Associated Press*. http://www.haaretz.com/hasen/spages/1035666.html.

Phalpot. "The Church of the Holy Sepulcher." Bible Places.com. www.bibleplaces.com/holysepulcher.htm.

"Pope in Visit to Religious Relic." *BBC News*. 1 September 2006. http://news.bbc.co.uk/2/hi/europe/5305592.stm.

Reilly, Wendell. "Dives." *The Catholic Encyclopedia*, vol. 5. http://www.newadvent.org/cathen/05048a.htm.

Electronic Works Cited

Rohrbaugh, Richard. "Honor and Shame: Core Values of the Biblical World." VHS. *Biblical Archaeology Society*, 2000.

"The Roman Army." http://library.thinkquest.org/22866/English/Leger.html.

"Study on the Physical Death of Christ." http://www.frugalsites.net/jesus/welcome.htm.

Taylor, Joan E. "Twenty-Four Hours That Changed the World Forever: An Easter Discussion." *Biblical Archaeology Review*. http://m www.bib-arch.org/onlineexclusives/easter-03.asp.

Ytrehus, Kjell. "Was Jesus Dead after Crucifixion?" *Tidsskrift for Den norske legeforening* No. 8 (March 2002): 833. http://www.tidsskriftet.no/?seks_id=526889.

CPSIA information can be obtained
at www.ICGtesting.com
Printed in the USA
BVOW08s1947310317
480002BV00001B/2/P